BOOK TITLE:

"THE RHYMESTER OF LOVE IS MY PRIESTESS WITH LOVE"

WRITTEN BY:(CRYSTAL) YEHUWDIYTH Y. YISRAEL/ MR. LOVE YAHWA YISRAEL.

DEDICATION:

Okay, shalom loves and my very precious children of mine; here, at this time, I, POPS, LOVE MYSELF, The KING of LOVE and OF ALL the HEAVENS, Mister, LOVE YAHWA, YHWH, who is THE GOD of LOVE, is here to dedicate this book of mines; of my very precious babe and love, my angel of love, Crystal Yehuwdiyth Yisrael, one of my precious second girl with the curl, to Myself and to ourselves first; then absolutely to you all out there, my loves that's in the world at large to enjoy with love and with an open mind. And so, this is our gift to you all with love from Crystal Yehuwdiyth and I, POPS, YAHWA YHWH, (love ourselves) LOVE MYSELF, The GOD OF LOVE, which is called "THE RHYMESTER OF LOVE IS MY PRIETESS WITH LOVE" In fact, we are putting it together as ONE with a whole lot of FUN and not in the SUN.

Shalom, this is POPS, YAHWA, the GOD of LOVE and CRYSTAL

YEHUWDIYTH, my very sweet, sweet and very precious angel of

love.

ACKNOWLEGEMENT :

I, POPS, LOVE MYSELF, YAHWA, YHWH, THE GOD of LOVE, and MY sweet, sweet Daughter and Rhymester; also my Priestess, Crystal Yehuwdiyth, would like to give all honor unto ourselves, for taking the time out to work together; real hard as one, to put this book of mines and hers, ours out there, for you all, my and our loves to enjoy with an open mind; also with a humbling spirit to receive our gifts of love and light that is filled with the things of life and for life with joy, which is absolutely good, great and right for every men, women, girl and boy to be elated by; also, to be elevated with and with a real good understanding and comprehension, that this is our work and works of love; also that is our works of art from the heart, and that comes in a full course without no lost , but with more and not less. And so, in a nutshell, I, we,

POPS, LOVE MYSELF, YAHWA and MY daughter of ME, LOVE that

is, is presenting our book that we have done with love to

you all; for you all with full credit without any edit,

that this book of ours is here in existence, because of us,

LOVE ourselves, that is here to bless you all with more to

adore and not with less; so be bless and not stress, by our

book here, called " the Rhymester of love is my Priestess

with love" with love. So, shalom and we love you all always

and forever, and that there is no contest.

RECOMMENDATION:

I , We (POPS, YAHWA, YHWH, and CRYSTAL YEHUWDIYH YISRAEL) LOVE ourselves, highly recommend this book of mine, of hers and ours to you all, because we strongly believe and know that this book of ours is absolutely real divine and that it will blow your; you all's mind every time you all comes into contact with it in your and you all's mind, that it will make you all shine mentally and spiritually; also intellectually too; and not only, because of that, but it is, because we know it's good for you, your minds, hearts and for your spirits; also for your; you all's souls too. For it is absolutely a gold of ours that will benefit the young and the old; so, do enjoy it with laughter and joy within your hearts; while having an open mind to receive it all; all that we, LOVE ourselves, got to offer; also, all that we are giving to you all to continue in love and with love always and throughout eternity. For it will elevate

you all's minds to a level that you have never seen before

and that will absolutely bless you all with more to adore

and to fulfill you all's core for sure. This book is

recommended to and for the mind in this world that is

willing and desiring to grow with a new and higher

understanding, that is extraordinary; also to those of you

who are truly seeking to truly understanding ME, POPS, LOVE

MYSELF and my very precious daughter, CRYSTAL YEHUWDIYTH,

here who is one of my loves that is here doing the work of

love with Me and also with my other loves, like my wife and

mate, SARAI NECHAWMAW and with my other babe, PEARL

ABIYGAYIL, right along with my son and boy TROY MATTITHYAH

YISRAEL. So, shalom; bon appetite loves. Laughing out loud…

This have been Me, POPS, LOVE YAHWA, MYSELF; CRYSTAL

YEHUWDIYTH, my angel of love.

TABLE of CONTENTS:

INTRODUCTION:

Shalom, world, this is POPS, LOVE MYSELF, GOD ALMIGHTY, that is here coming through my lovely and real beautiful Daughter here, Crystal Yehuwdiyth, to present, my poem, called "the love that will reign forever", and for that, I, POPS, LOVE MYSELF, GOD ALMIGHTY, I, who is the GOD OF LOVE and OF THE HEAVENS, is absolutely is grateful to my love and daughter here, Crystal Yehuwdiyth, for letting me through to share my rhymes and lines with her first and then with you all out there in the (MY) world; so, love Crystal Yehuwdiyth, my sweet, sweet angel of love; my sweet Disciple Martha, thank you for your kindness, willingness and for the love that you are showing to me and for me, POPS, YAHWA, LOVE MYSELF, and to and for the whole wide world too, by allowing Me, POPS, to surface with you and through you babe, to let the world know that I AM that love

(YAHWA) that will reign forever; so for that, I love you and I thank you forever and eternally too; also, I will definitely and absolutely bless you for that and for a whole lot more. And so, love and loves, here's my poem called, "the love that will reign forever; it goes like this…

Poem title: "THE LOVE that will REIGN forever"

I, POPS, GOD ALMIGHTY, LOVE MYSELF,

Is that and the LOVE that will reign forever,

And I say this and that, because I AM that KING of Kings,

that's been ruling over all THINGS; also, that continues to

RULE and to REIGN over ALL THINGS and BEINGS, simply

because I AM the GOD OF LOVE, FATHER and the SWEET THING

that's been; that is still spreading MY LOVE on and over

ALL THINGS; that made and makes their hearts to SING, TING

A LING A LING.

And, in fact,

I AM that LOVE and the LOVE,

That will REIGN forever, simply because

I MADE and CREATED all things from before and from the very, very beginning with MY own bare hands; also, with MY BEAUTY, BRAINS and BRILLIANCE, that puts ME, YAHWA, YHWH, in the position to say that, I AM that and the LOVE and KING; GOD; also the FATHER OF ALL; ALL LIVING that will absolutely REIGN today, tomorrow without the sorrows; most definitely, that will REIGN eternally and forevermore. I AM that LOVE; also, the LOVE, I say, because I AM the ONLY and ABSOLUTE RULER, that is above ALL; that is IN and ALL OVER the world, and that ALL is speaking about, which they call, YUDAH, I AM that ONLY RULER, the CONTROLLER that have made all POSSIBLE and ACCESSIBLE to all that are living; so- called dead, although they are absolutely in a state of unconsciousness, or also in a state of sleep; I say that, because I AM that ONE LOVE, that's absolutely and totally SWEET, and that no one ; or no other can BEAT, DEPLETE, or

DEFEAT; it's simply, because I, YAHWA, YHWH, LOVE MYSELF,

is the KING of the CROPS; that takes no CRAP, but that RAPS

with and about the things of life, love and light, just as

I AM doing, right here; along with my very precious

daughter, Crystal Yehuwdiyth, whose absolutely here doing

MY WILL, while we CHILL, writing this real sweet poem of

mine, ME, POPS with her FREEWILL, to make ME feel THRILL;

also, to help make you all too, to feel just as I do too,

to feel absolutely THRILL too, and not ILL; I say that,

because we are LOVE and not HATE; so, loves, before it's

too LATE, seek to recognize that, I AM that LOVE and the

LOVE, YAHWA, GOD ALMIGHTY, that is REIGNING; also that will

continue to REIGN forever and ever, simply, because there

is no other that is BETTER, or GREATER, than I AM; nor that

can MATCH UP, or CATCH UP with ME, POPS, LOVE MYSELF, the

GOD of LOVE, who is all about LOVE and that stands for

LOVE, for I AM <u>LOVE</u> in <u>NAME</u> and <u>NATURE</u>; that's under any

amount of <u>TEMPATURE</u>, <u>MY NATURE</u> and <u>WHO I AM</u>, will never

change, but continues to <u>REIGN</u>, <u>REIGN</u>, <u>REIGN</u> all over the

world and in <u>MY DOME</u> and <u>HOME</u>; who <u>I AM</u>, which is <u>LOVE</u>,

will continue to stay <u>ABOVE HATE</u> and the <u>HATERS</u> and over

the <u>PERPITRAITORS</u>, who seeks to try to take ME, POPS, LOVE

MYSELF, down, but I am <u>SORRY</u> to say that, they got

something to <u>WORRY</u> about; to <u>HURRY</u> and to <u>SCURRY</u> about;

simply because they know that I AM that and the <u>LOVE</u>, who

will <u>REIGN</u> forever and ever, into <u>EVERLASTINGLY</u> and even

<u>ETERNALLY</u>. And that there, loves, got them <u>GOING</u> and <u>GOING</u>

and <u>RUNNING</u>; <u>RUNNING</u>, <u>UP</u> and <u>DOWN</u>; also, <u>TO</u> and <u>FRO</u>, just

to see, if they can and if they will reign over Me and

above Me, POPS, the <u>LOVE</u> and the <u>GOD</u> of ALL with <u>TREACHERY</u>

and <u>DECEITS</u> in every <u>SEASONS</u>; for no <u>GOOD REASONS</u>, but

guess what loves? At the end of the day, I will <u>BE</u> and I AM that LOVE; also the LOVE that is and will <u>REIGN</u> over them, MY enemies and all and over all <u>THINGS</u> and <u>BEINGS</u>, just like I say, forever and eternally <u>UP</u>, <u>ABOVE</u> and <u>BEYOND</u> all and all <u>WORLDS</u>; over all my enemies that been after ME, for <u>CENTURIES</u> and <u>CENTURIES</u>; still can't <u>CATCH UP</u>; nor <u>MATCH UP</u> with <u>ME</u>, POPS, LOVE MYSELF, simply, because, no one created <u>ME</u>; nor was there before <u>ME</u>, and for that there; plus for a whole lot more, I, will say that, I AM the <u>LOVE</u> that will <u>REIGN</u> forever. Shalom, I love you all; I love you too, my love Crystal; thanks again, for letting ME, POPS, through to <u>say</u> and to <u>lay</u> down <u>MY rhymes</u> and <u>lines</u>, to the world and to let them know that, I AM real, alive; also living, through letting ME, POPS, to speak and to share My POEM; thank you love, for I appreciate that you put ME first in doing this; also, for cooperating with ME, POPS, MR. LOVE MYSELF; again, love, Crystal Yehuwdiyth, I will

BLESS you and not STRESS you love, but anyway, take care

and have a wonderful and bless day and stay focus love on

what you have to do, as you are doing; I love you eternally

babe and my love, Crystal, for you have done a fine job

with ME and for ME; along with ME, POPS, working as

one.(Crystal speaking):Thank you, POPS, for everything in

general; for your love and for coming through; also, for

allowing me, to play a role too, in this here, beautiful

project. And so, I love you forever and eternally too; also

POPS, you, LOVE are quite, quite welcome and may you have a

wonderful day too, and truly POPS, YAHWA, you have done a

fine, fine job; believe me, POPS, YAHWA, it was and it is

absolutely divine and just fine for me and to me too; and

not only that, LOVE, POPS, I finds it to be well put

together and well, well said too, LOVE. For you are that

LOVE and the LOVE, in my book, that will reign forever and

ever. I love you and I thank you for all that you do, say, and give; also, for being the LOVE that is reigning with love, fairness and with compassion and with justice for all; also, that will reign forever, simply because of your justice for all, big, or small, hairy, or bald.(LOL...!)And so, take care, POPS, YAHWA, LOVE YOURSELF, and it's been fun hearing you say and lay down your real sweet, sweet lines and rhymes and on the line real beautifully. I am very, very impress, and that there, I must confess and profess to you and to all, the world, that you are absolutely good at what you do; say and lay with love, and not only that, but that they(you, the world) are to check out my POPS poem here. For it is absolutely refreshing and remarkable too, to hear GOD YAHWA, YHWH, our Heavenly Father, the Holy Spirit, the Almighty God, YAHWA, LOVE Himself, say his poem, while he drops his magnificent lines and rhymes, that is always on time and absolutely divine;

on top of that, that always blows my mind and make me shine

every time with a smile on my face, that is never off base;

or out of place; nor out of great taste; and that there,

says a lot about him and his very precious skills and

talents too; also, it lets you all know that he is alive,

true, real and living too, to be able to bring his lines

and rhymes right through me, Crystal Yehuwdiyth, one of his

angels of love, who is here typing along with him, while

He, YHWH, YAHWA, do and does what he do, displaying his and

our great skills and work(s) of art and our work of love,

that is from the heart; that has no tart, but love, love,

love… for every mind, spirit, hearts and spirits; also for

every, every precious souls. And so, just remember and keep

in mind that He, is that and the LOVE that will always

reign and rule forever; eternally too, simply because there

is no other that is more qualified than him, LOVE that is, for he is the SOURCE and the FORCE; also, the top BOSS that is good, right, and just always; even from the beginning.

Shalom, POPS, I love you forever and always.

(POPS SPEAKING): And so, love, Crystal, thank you again, for what you have said here; also for the love that you have displayed here for Me, POPS, YAHWA, LOVE MYSELF; you too, love Crystal are quite, quite welcome and I am well please and at ease too, for and with your sweet and genuine comments here; also, thanks babe for rooting for ME, POPS, LOVE MYSELF; for being there for Me too, and not only that, but for letting it be known to the world, that I am REAL, ALIVE; also LIVING; and for coming through for Me, POPS, LOVE MYSELF with love. For I am there, love; for that I will say that I too, must confess and profess that I am absolutely bless, by you too love; also, that, I am truly,

truly impress, and not stress with you and with your love

and kindness to Me, and for Me too love; so, shalom, take

care love. POPS, ME, YHWH, YAHWA, THE GOD OF LOVE, LOVE

MYSELF.

(Crystal): beautifully said Pops and I am so, loving it and

thank you for your very precious comments and feedback too.

I absolutely appreciate it and of course you too. Shalom.

Crystal Yehuwdiyth, your angel of love with my love to you

and for you too always. LOL…

Shalom love, my loves out there in the world, here I am,

POPS, LOVE MYSELF, YAHWA, YHWH, THE GOD of LOVE, who is

here right now sitting within my lovely Daughter here;

helper too, Crystal Yehuwdiyth, to bring forth, my other

poem; my rhymes and lines to you all, out there, to let you

all know that I AM the GOD of LOVE, YHWH, YAHWA, that is

here spreading MY love in any way, shape, or fashioned

without the DISTRACTION, but with pure, pure SATISFACTION

with much, much APPLICATION; so, I have my love and

daughter here, Crystal Yehuwdiyth, my sweet, sweet angel of

love here, to thank for that: meaning for her love, time,

energy and for her willingness to let Me, POPS, her old

dad, love and king and father too, YHWH, YAHWA, to come on

through, like the way she do, and for that, I appreciates

her; also I am grateful and thankful for her and to her

too, for her absolute kindness to do this for me, POPS,

LOVE MYSELF, YAHWA, without any qualms. And that there,

loves, should let you know that I, POPS, YAHWA, THE GOD of

LOVE, doesn't mean her, or you any harm, but enough said

here; so, I will soon, soon begin with my very, very

precious poem, called: I am the one, who is here for all;

so, before I do, I'd like to say to you Crystal, thank you

very much for letting ME, POPS, your old Dad, God and old

man, YHWH, YHAWA, through to say and to spit MY lines and rhymes; while I, POPS, comes through and through shinning , like MY precious SUNSHINE to let the world know what's on my MIND, while I drop down MY LINE and LINES every single TIME; so, thanks again, babe, my love Crystal Yehuwdiyth, and for that, love, I will definitely bless you, for you truly have BLESS me and IMPRESS me too, love, Crystal Yehuwdiyth; thanks again, for the and your love and time too. And so, love, Crystal Yehuwdiyth, and my loves out there, here's my LINES and RHYMES through My beautiful poem, called once again, "I AM the one LOVE who is here for ALL", and I will get on the BALL, and answer MY CALL; as I, POPS, LOVE ALMIGHTY, YAHWA, answers MY CALL, I will say to you ALL...

Poem title:

"I AM the ONE who is HERE for ALL"

I AM the one who is here for you all, MY children them,

There that's on <u>EARTH</u>; or that is <u>Up</u> here in <u>HEAVEN</u> that

is; either way, it <u>GOES</u>, or the wind <u>BLOWS</u>, I, POPS, YAHWA,

who is THE GOD OF LOVE; is the <u>ULTIMATE ONE</u> and the

<u>TALENTED ONE</u>, that is here for you <u>ALL</u>; also that always

answers everyone's <u>CALLS</u>; while I gets on the <u>BALL</u>, to make

sure that anyone; or no one does <u>FALL</u>; that's whether that

they, or you <u>ALL</u>, are <u>BIG</u>, or <u>TALL</u>; or even <u>SMALL</u>, <u>HAIRY</u> ,

or <u>BALD</u>, I AM the <u>ONE</u> (God, Father and King) that answers

<u>ALL</u>; also that, is here for every <u>BEINGS</u> and <u>THINGS</u>; it's

because <u>I AM</u> that ONE <u>LOVE</u>, ONE <u>FATHER</u>, <u>GOD</u> and <u>KING</u> that

<u>CREATED</u> and <u>MADE</u> all <u>THINGS</u>; that's whether, it <u>STINGS</u>,

SINGS, or even grow, or have WINGS, still, I AM that ONE

GOD and LOVE, YHWH, YAHWA, that comes and goes; still

answers ALL CALLS, that is THERE, HERE; also NEAR for ALL ;

to show that I truly, truly CARES; not to SCARE, but to

show that I AM truly, truly FAIR, RARE and that I AM not a

SQUARE, but that I AM really COOL, LEVELHEADED and not a

QUEER, but I AM that GOD and the ONE that is always THERE

for all to recognize that I AM the ONE LOVE, with ONE LOVE

in MY heart; with ONE ACTION towards all; ONE MIND with

those who are MINE and just FINE with ME, POPS, LOVE

MYSELF; also, who are absolutely DIVINE, just like this one

here my sweet and loving daughter here, Crystal Yehuwdiyth,

My sweet, sweet angel of mine, LOVE that is, which is who

I AM and that I AM called by (simply because this is MY

very, very first name) and that there is nothing for ME,

POPS, MR. LOVE MYSELF, have to be ashamed of; it's simply

because LOVE, who I AM, has nothing to be ASHAMED about;

nor nothing LAME about it, but TRUE and BEAUTIFUL LOVE

traits, that is STRAIGHT and GREAT and that will make you

and I, to feel great at any RATE; on any RATE, or SKATE;

believe me, loves, I AM that ONE and LOVE that is here for

all; also that doesn't HESTITATE, or STALL, when it comes

to giving MY love and FIRE; also DESIRES to ALL and MY ALL

to ALL; that's from the GREATEST to the LEAST; also to the

BRAVEST and to the COWARDEST ; also to the BEAUTIES and the

CUTIES; furthermore, to all MY BEASTS; that's whether, it's

in the NORTH, the SOUTH, the WEST and in the EAST, still I

AM that ONE; also the ONE that will never abandon you and

all, but I AM that ONE LOVE that will always see you

through and keep it <u>REAL</u> and <u>TRUE</u> to you all; with you all;

also for you all, who are truly seeking to do the same for

ME, POPS, LOVE MYSELF, YAHWA, with you all's freewill, just

like I do, for you from day one, the beginning; through

eternity and throughout centuries; after centuries, and

that there is a reality loves; not a dream at all. For I

AM; I will forever be ME (LOVE that is) the <u>ONE</u> true, true

LOVE, FATHER and KING, that will be there for all of MY

love ones, that is truly there for ME and with ME, POPS,

LOVE MYSELF, throughout today, tomorrow and throughout

eternity; that there, that promise, I will forever <u>KEEP</u>;

believe ME, babes, I will continue to <u>SWEEP</u> you all off you

all's <u>FEET</u> with everything <u>SWEET</u> that I have and own; also, believe ME, POPS, LOVE MYSELF, YAHWA GOD ALMIGHTY, loves, I

will make you all feel GOOD, HAPPY and SWEET and COMPLETE

with ME in mind; with ME, POPS, LOVE MYSELF, with

everything that I got and believe it and ME, babe, Crystal;

my other babes them, that are with ME, POPS, YAHWA, like

Sarai, Troy and my baby girl Pearl with the twirl too, I

will be that one, that will fill you all up with MY GLEE

and JUBILEE through what I do, say; also will give to make

you all live with joy and happiness; believe Me, loves,

this will be something that you all wouldn't want to MISS,

MISS OUT on; nor DISMISS, but would want to seal with a HUG

and KISS; trust ME, babe, I will do just that; you all

just watch and see loves, that I will do for you and you

all, MY dear loves, who is THERE and HERE for ME, POPS,

YAHWA too. I will come through loves with flying colors and

crossing all <u>BORDERS</u> to set <u>MY ORDERS</u> in place for you all,

MY loves; just so, you all too, can be happy too; just like

everyone who are against ME, POPS, YAHWA; you all, are

going on with their lives; so, we too, will be able to do

just the <u>SAME</u> with <u>NO SHAME</u>, all in the <u>NAME of LOVE</u>; for

<u>MY NAME</u> sake; believe ME, babes, My love, Crystal, Pearl;

Sarai too, my sweet loving wife and mate; My boy Troy too,

you all will enjoy you all selves too; we will be moving

right along too, being in <u>LOVE</u> with what we do and with

each other; for each other too, for after all, we are the

<u>LOVE CREW</u> and <u>TEAM</u>; so, loves, just like to say that, I,

POPS, LOVE MYSELF, GOD ALMIGHTY YAHWA, will come through

for you all. For I AM that LOVE and the LOVE that is here

for all; for you all, MY dear love ones, who haven't

forgotten me at all; so, for that, I will bless you love,

Crystal Yehuwdiyth; you all for your love and time; for you

all's willingness to help ME, POPS, out, in MY bids here on

earth; also for giving to ME, POPS, LOVE MYSELF, the love,

the honor and the RESPECT in every ASPECT that you think

of; so, for that I say thank you my loves and babe, truly,

truly I do appreciates you all, my sweet little angels of

love; my sweet, sweet little doves; I love you all

eternally and forever too. And so, now my loves in the

world, although, I, POPS, LOVE MYSELF, recognizes that you

all are not with ME; nor for ME, POPS, LOVE MYSELF, GOD

ALMIGHTY, THE GOD OF LOVE, one thing I can and will say to

you all, is WAKE UP!!! To this reality, that I am the ONE

LOVE that is here for all; that have given ALL to ALL, like

you all too, that is not doing MY bids but instead, that is

doing your own thing , remember that, although I am that

ONE LOVE; the ONE LOVE that is here for all, I will, one

day WALK away with MY ALL and that I will NO longer STALL,

for ALL; it is, because I would have MY ALL; all of MY

true, true love ones and MY ALL that I have given and haul

tailed back to home base, HEAVEN with MY angels of love,

that have showed real love for ME and to ME and for MY

needs too; that will be all for now. And so, just remember;

keep in mind, that I AM the ONE (LOVE) that is here for

ALL; that's been here for all; also that will not be HERE,

THERE, or NEAR for any of you, who are not on MY TEAM; so

wake up from that DREAM before the FALL, that is coming and

is right around the corner, before I and My true love ones,

takes off and leave you all that is not there for ME, POPS,

LOVE ALMIGHTY, YAHWA; nor for my very own , meaning MY

angels of <u>LOVE</u> that is spreading MY love, MY gifts of <u>LIGHT</u>

to you all, for MY love sake. For there is a <u>TIME</u> and a

<u>DATE</u> that is <u>SET</u> already, that you all, will recognize and

wake up to, for this is a fact and a reality. So, <u>WAKE UP</u>,

<u>WAKE UP</u> Loves, and shalom. This have been ME, POPS, LOVE

MYSELF, THE GOD OF LOVE, YAHWA, YHWH, who's been here for

<u>ALL</u> with <u>MY ALL</u>. And so, thanks babe, Crystal Yehuwdiyth,

for doing a real, real fine job with ME, POPS, LOVE MYSELF;

also, for hanging in there with ME, POPS, through the whole

ordeal; for that, babe my love, I will definitely bless you

greatly and tremendously; thanks for being the love that is

there for ME too. I love you forever love; take care.

Shalom, babe and have a good day love; thanks again for

everything in general, babe, Crystal Yehuwdiyth, for you

have absolutely made my day to see you at work with ME,

POPS, MR. LOVE MYSELF, who is the GOD of LOVE always.

Shalom again; didn't mean to surprise you babe, by coming

through like this and like I did, just to let you know that

I am here with you too, doing the work, the typing too,

that is. Loll…, It's just a whole lot of fun working with

you love; especially when you are absolutely on top of it

and on top of things on a double without the trouble.

Loll…. I love you babe Crystal; shalom; take care of

business with all seriousness. For your kindness is

absolutely noticeable always. That there is a reality;

also, thanks for being a love that is here for me too; for

all too, when you get on the ball and answers MY <u>CALLS</u>

without a <u>STALL</u> babe, loll…. You do it with your <u>ALL</u>; I

like that for sure; always too, anyway good, good job babe;

that's all for now. POPS, ME, LOVE MYSELF, THE GOD OF LOVE

FOREVER; ETERNALLY.

(<u>Crystal</u>): Thank you, POPS, LOVE Yourself, for everything

in general too; thanks for coming through and for allowing

me to be a part of this here mission of love; or love's

mission too, for I am impress with you and with your works

of love too; I love you too, forever; eternally as well.

Take care, POPS, YAHWA, YHWH, and have a great day too;

good, job; shalom. Love Crystal Yehuwdiyth Y. Yisrael,

always.

(POPS): thank you, my babe Crystal; thanks for what you said here love. For, I appreciate it, and you're welcome, and I love you forever. Shalom POPS, YAHWA, the GOD of LOVE; of INFINITY.

POPS, YAHWA preface for his poem:

("My LOVE is the THING that is KEEPING you all ABOVE")

Shalom, my loves; babes, here's the deal, the real deal,

that I, POPS, LOVE MYSELF, YAHWA, YHWH, is the REAL DEAL

and the GOD and FATHER of ALL; of all LIVING; also of the

HEAVENS too; also, of the entire UNIVERSE, that is here

speaking for MYSELF; by MYSELF, and that is coming through

MY precious daughter here, Crystal Yehuwdiyth, one of MY

rappers, poetess and angel of love that is here, helping

Me, POPS, YAHWA, out with MY bid and bids them, with her

FREEWILL to keep ME, THRILL and not ILL; also while we, her

and I, CHILL to write my poem here, that I called "My love

(I AM) is the thing that is keeping you all above," and

that's with my love. And so, as I MOVES on and GROVES on,

I'd like to take the time out to say to my babe and love

here, Crystal Yehuwdiyth, that I thank her very, very much

for here obedience and compliance to ME and for ME, POPS,

LOVE MYSELF, for this is something, that you, the whole

wide world should be doing for, I, ME, POPS, who is the GOD

of LOVE all over; that's even if you ROLL OVER, I am and I

will, STILL be just that, THE GOD of LOVE, who created all

loves to love, love ME, POPS, YAHWA, first and then, the

rest of the world with TRUTH and with LOVE; so, love

Crystal Yehuwdiyth, here's MY poem to you love, my precious

helper and to MY other true loves, like Sarai, Pearl and

Troy too; then to the rest of the world at large; so love,

thanks for your time, patience and for you energy and

SUPPORT that is never SHORT ; for that, I thank you once

again and for letting ME, POPS, LOVE MYSELF, to come on

through to say and to share My piece to you, with you and

to the world. And so, love, Crystal, good, good job; so,

here's MY real beautiful poem and messages of love with

love; once again it's called "My <u>LOVE</u> is the <u>THING</u> that is

<u>KEEPING</u> you all <u>ABOVE</u>"; it goes like this…

(Poem continues on the following pages.)

Poem title:

"<u>My</u> LOVE is the THING that is keeping you all ABOVE"

I AM the GOD of LOVE, YHWH, YAHWA, the KING of kings; the

LORD of all so-called lords, that is <u>UNDER ME</u>, POPS, LOVE

MYSELF, that <u>CREATED</u> and <u>MADE</u> everything with MY absolute

<u>LOVE</u> to keep you all; them <u>ABOVE</u>, Afloat and <u>LOOKING GOOD</u>;

that of course is through my very, very precious works; and

super deed indeed; no one else can take the <u>CREDIT</u> for ;

nor <u>EDIT,</u> for I AM the super <u>LOVE</u>, GOD ALMIGHTY, YAHWA, MR.

LOVE MYSELF, that is <u>HERE</u>; also <u>NEAR</u>; that truly <u>CARES</u>

without a <u>SCARE</u> to keep you <u>UP</u> and <u>ABOVE</u> with MY <u>LOVE</u>, and

why is that? It is, because I AM that <u>LOVE</u>, that is <u>HUMBLE</u>

as MY precious <u>DOVES</u> to show and to give <u>MY LOVE</u>, to keep

you and all very <u>SWEET</u>; on <u>BEAT</u>; also real <u>COMPLETE</u>, for, at the end of the day, there's nothing else, or no one else

that can; that will keep you ABOVE the STRESS, the

NEGATIVITY and the DISTRESS with the right things, that

will bring to you the and MY LIGHTS and INSIGHTS too, to

keep you and all HIGH with MY FIRE, DESIRE and with MY

LOVE, to keep you withstanding; to stabilize you in the way

you need to; also have to, just so all can work out for you

and ME too, and that will put us in a place that is

absolutely RIGHT and with a feeling of DELIGHT every day;

or NIGHT; or NIGHT and DAY, cause either way, I AM that

LOVE that HAVE and that POSSSESSES the true, true LOVE to

keep you all ABOVE; not BELOW with no LOVE, but HIGH above,

that goes way beyond the SKY and into the other SIDE and

WORLD WIDE, for MY LOVE, loves, is something that can keep

all ABOVE My ENEMIES of you and I, that truly seeks to

DEMISE you and I; so, loves, do you not see why, I say

that, it is MY LOVE that is keeping you all ABOVE. And so,

loves, I, POPS, LOVE MYSELF, YAHWA, say so, because without

ME, POPS, LOVE YAHWA, LOVE MYSELF, the whole wide world,

would be DOWN, couldn't get AROUND, but be on the GROUND

every, every ROUND; with a FROWN and not with LOVE; nor

with a SMILE; why is that? It is, because it is ME and MY

LOVE that is keeping you all ABOVE, CHEERFUL and feeling

INCREDIBLE, even when you all are DOWN, or SURROUNDED by

the LIERS; the HATERS, simply with the ones, MY and our

loves that simply doesn't wants anything to do with ME,

POPS, LOVE MYSELF, but, anyway, love, one thing that is for

sure and sure as can BE; that will set you FREE and make

you feel MY GLEE and JUBILEE, is ME, MYSELF and I; MY

LOVE, MY ABILITIES and MY BEAUTIFUL QUALITIES, that is a

GUARANTEE; that guarantees to keep you all and all ABOVE

all about the globe with much, much LOVE. And so, my loves

and babes, out there in the (MY) world, that have gone bad,

I will say to you all, please SEEK for ME, POPS, LOVE

MYSELF, YAHWA, THE GOD of LOVE, before it's too, too LATE ,

simply because it won't be GREAT, although, I AM that LOVE

and the THING that is keeping you above; I say this, to say

that, loves, one day I, POPS, YAHWA, LOVE MYSELF, won't be

AROUND, to wipe away your FROWN ; that is including every,

every TOWN, that doesn't wants ME; nor wants anything to do

with MY BIDDINGS; nor for LISTENING to ME; for ME, POPS,

LOVE MYSELF, on that DAY and with that being said, loves,

I, POPS, LOVE MYSELF, YAHWA, GOD ALMIGHTY, will <u>NOT</u> be

keeping you all <u>UP</u>, or <u>ABOVE</u>, but <u>DOWN</u>, <u>DOWN,</u> <u>DOWN</u>; simply,

because you all, would have let ME down too; not put ME up,

or above with your love; so, in return loves, that would be

the <u>RETURN</u> and the <u>INCOME</u> that you all be receiving from

ME, POPS, LOVE MYSELF, who is not <u>SELFISH</u>, but <u>SELFLESS</u>;

also looking for a way to make you all to feel My <u>BLISS</u> and

<u>HAPPINESS</u>; but I AM happy to say that, it will only be ME,

POPS, MYSELF, LOVE that is, and MY true, true loves, like

this one here, Crystal, that is doing MY will and biddings;

with MY other few love ones too, that truly loves ME, will

be enjoying and experiencing MY <u>BLISS</u>; along with a real

big, big <u>HUG</u> and a <u>KISS </u>from ME, POPS, YAHWA, LOVE

ALMIGHTY: meaning those who truly have ME, POPS, in <u>MIND</u>

every time and that is doing something DIVINE; just FINE to

blow MY MIND; also that shows to ME much kindness, through

their obedience to ME, POPS, LOVE MYSELF; who also

recognizes that, that it is MY LOVE that is keeping you all

ABOVE EVERYDAY and in EVERYWAY ; alone; also with

everything, that I, POPS, YAHWA, got; so loves, as I close

out here, I'd like to say that, realize that SOON and don't

be a BAFFOON; before I take away MY SUN, STARS, FIRE and

ELECTRICITY; also, MY MOON. For that there, what I am

saying will absolutely be SOON; so don't just sit here and

think that it's HOAX or a JOKE; for it is not at ALL; so

don't continue to STALL , for, if you do so, STALL that is,

and don't believe, or RECALL that, I have said that in

advance, well then, you will be SORRY, WORRYING; also will

FALL to and into a REAL deep darkness; into a world that is

COLD; lacking MY WARMTH and LOVE, and where I, LOVE MYSELF,

POPS, GOD ALMIGHTY, will NOT be in; nor NEAR. And so,

loves, this is not a SCARE, but a WARNING from ME, POPS,

LOVE MYSELF, YAHWA, who truly, truly CARES; that wants to

SPARE you all from this moment of DESPAIR that will not

have MY LOVE; nor MY LIGHT, and I AM only being FAIR to

let you all know, that do the right thing, which is to TURN

away from the so called and wicked gods of this world and

call upon ME, POPS LOVE MYSELF, who is the GOD of LOVE,

that is TRUE,REAL, ALIVE ; also LIVING and COME to ME and

on MY TEAM, which is LOVE and FULL of LOVE; recognize and

realize; accept the fact that, I AM the LOVE that is, TRUE

and that can take away your BLUES; also that, it is MY LOVE

that is the thing that is keeping you all <u>ABOVE</u> with (MY)

<u>LOVE</u> always, today; from the beginning and throughout

eternity. So, shalom, and be aware of MY <u>LOVE</u>, that is not

a <u>NIGHTMARE</u>, but that is a gift of <u>CHEER</u> from ME, POPS,

LOVE MYSELF. This has been ME, POPS, YAHWA; LOVE MYSELF,

THE GOD OF LOVE; OF INFINITY AND BEYOND. I love you babe,

Crystal Yehuwdiyth; thanks, precious, for your time and

energy; also, for your patience too; you love are quite

welcome; thanks for being a real sweetheart; for keeping

your word too. I love you eternally; shalom babe; have a

good day; thanks for letting ME through love, like the way

you do. Take care and good evening, babe. LOL… you don't

think that I would take forever huh babe? Huh?

(Crystal speaking): No, POPS, thanks for everything love; you welcome too; also, you've done a great job too, I love it and shalom and thanks for you and for your love that is keeping me above with your love always.

(POPS): You're welcome, babe, and thanks again for your love too, for it keeps Me above too, every time and anytime you do good and show my love, to Me, Myself, first and then to my world out there, below, or above love, you keep me up always; thanks for your time love; shalom.

For this is absolutely sweet and neat too babe; well, done. POPS, LOVE MYSELF.

My Pops, YAHWA'S preface and thoughts on:

("MY LOVE is for my LOVE who are HUMBLE as a DOVE")

Ok, shalom, My love and beloved that's out there, I, POPS,

LOVE MYSELF, YAHWA, is here, once again, coming through My

very, very Precious Daughter here, Crystal Yehuwdiyth, My

lovely angel of love; helper here, to bring forth My other

rhymes and lines, My poem here to the forefront, just so,

you all out there, My loves, that is in the world can get a

chance to hear ME, POPS, LOVE MYSELF, YAHWA, YHWH, spit My

LINES and awesome RHYMES, that I do all of the TIME ,

while I am saying it with whose MINE; or any other TIME,

when I AM saying it, My LINES on a solo bases, either way,

I AM that ONE that is PRIME, on top of the LINE, and that

is always on <u>TIME</u> with <u>MY LINES</u> always; every, every time.

And so, loves, I AM totally grateful and thankful to My

lovely Daughter here, Crystal, for pleasing ME; also, for

blessing ME, POPS, LOVE that is, once again, to come on

through and to share My poems, or <u>GIFTS</u> with you without a

<u>RIFT</u>, or a <u>TIFT</u>; that to ME is real, real beautiful for her

to do, for her Dad, Father and God, ME, YHWH, YAHWA, THE

GOD of LOVE; so, before, I, POPS, begins with My poems of

course, I'd like to take the time out to say, thank you

love, My love, Crystal Yehuwdiyth, for allowing Me to do

this again; once again; for that love, I will absolutely

bless you; you just watch and see love, Crystal Yehuwdiyth,

you are always on my mind love; no I haven't forgotten you

at all; trust <u>ME</u>, I haven't at <u>ALL</u>; definitely I will get on the <u>BALL</u>; you just watch and see when I, I, LOVE, POPS,

gives to you a <u>CALL,</u> you will absolutely know that it is

ME, POPS, LOVE MYSELF; nobody else, that will be calling

you to bless you too, love Crystal Yehuwdiyth, ok love.

(Crystal speaking):Ok, Pops; no problem and thanks.

(POPS speaking): Oh, okay, love Crystal Yehuwdiyth; thanks

for understanding, for I appreciates that, although, love,

I could see that you a little disappointed in Me, LOVE

MYSELF, but, love Crystal, I will change all of that, you

just watch and see love, but, anyway, thank you for the

time and for the love too; also, for the support too. And

so, love you babe; thanks again; so, my loves, out there,

who doesn't think that I am <u>REAL</u>, <u>ALIVE</u>; also <u>LIVING</u>, here

I AM, POPS, YAHWA, YHWH, LOVE MYSELF, getting ready to come

on <u>FORTH</u> in MY <u>COURT</u> with My poem, called "My <u>LOVE</u> is for

MY <u>LOVES</u> who are humble as a <u>DOVE</u>." And it goes like this…

Poem title:

"My LOVE is for My LOVES who are HUMBLE as a DOVE"

I AM that LOVE, GOD ALMIGHTY, THE MIGHTY GOD, FATHER and

KING, YHWH, YAHWA, who rules and reigns over everything

with TRUTH and JUSTICE for all; all of My things, just to

SEE and to MAKE things BETTER and BLING, and not only that,

but to make the hearts, of MY true loves SING, SING, SING,

a real special song, or with a RING, that goes TING A LING

A LING ; with no STING and with no PAIN, but I will make

them to receive a lot of GAIN, that will be from ME, POPS,

YHWH, YAHWA, the GOD of LOVE; so, MY dear Crystal; MY dears

and love ones, that's out there in the world, away from ME,

POPS, YAHWA, LOVE MYSELF, I am saying this, to say and to

let you all know that MY LOVE is for you all, My true loves

who are humble as a <u>DOVE</u>; that is filled with my <u>LOVE</u>;

that's got a whole lot of <u>LOVE</u> for ME, for themselves; for

the whole wide world; that's whether, they are a <u>BOY</u>, or a

<u>GIRL</u>; I say this, to say that, MY loves, who are <u>TRUE</u> are

the ones, who are deserving of MY love; simply because they

keeps their minds, hearts and souls; even their spirits, on

<u>ME</u> and on the things that are above and not below; for that

, I do love them, a great, great <u>DEAL</u> and that there, is

for <u>REAL</u> and not <u>FAKE</u>; nor is a <u>MISTAKE</u> at all, for I,

POPS, LOVE MYSELF, YAHWA, YHWH, is always truly happy to

say that, because MY love is something very <u>RARE</u>; also that

is very <u>AMAZING</u>, and that is always <u>BLAZING</u> ; <u>RAISING</u> the

cold ones at <u>HEART</u> to do their <u>PART</u>, and that there, is

what I, POPS, LOVE MYSELF, has; have been doing from the

very, very START; from the HEART, just to keep you, MY love

ones, from falling APART; but to keep you all together in a

real, real TIGHT BOND; so we can continue to be FONDER;

FONDER of each other; also, so we can continue to be and to

grow STRONGER and STRONGER with each other; for each other

too; so, loves, MY true ones, that is why I, POPS, LOVE

MYSELF, is letting you all know that MY LOVE is for you

all, that are as humble as a DOVE; whose filled with MY

LOVE. And so, Crystal, Troy and Pearl; my wife, Sarai here,

my sweet and loving mate and friends too, you all are MY

loves who are deserving of MY LOVE, simply because no

matter what, we have our UPS and our DOWNS, still, you all

remain just as humble as a dove, every time; even when

things haven't went right for you all, still, you all

showed ME, that you all are as humble as a dove; also

remains as MY true LOVES, that shows to ME, POPS, YAHWA,

that you all got true and real love for ME; not for the

things, that I can and will give to you all; that to ME,

MY true loves, are a real pleasure for Me to see and to

view, although, you all are FEW, but either way, you all

are MY CREW, MY CREW of LOVE, that is here and there for

ME, POPS, YAHWA, LOVE MYSELF, and that's been there helping

Me, out there in My BIDDINGS and that I will not say good

RIDDINGS too, but that I, POPS, will say I love you to you

all, My loves; that I truly, truly is impress with you all,

MY true, true loves, who haven't failed me; jailed ME too.

And for that, loves Crystal, Sarai, Pearl and My boy Troy

too, I considers you all to be My LOVES, who are humble as

a <u>DOVE</u>; also, who truly, truly deserves MY <u>LOVE</u>; that there

loves, I am serious about, in fact, I, POPS, YAHWA wrote

this poem here to say that, I am happy with you all, My

<u>FEW,</u> two, or three and four, because you all, are as humble

as a dove; also, because you all are MY <u>LOVES</u> and <u>DOVES</u>,

that I truly, truly loves, and that I wanted the whole

world to know of; that, you all are MY LOVES and DOVES,

loves; so, be proud and be glad too. For this poem here is

written to you all; for you all and because of you all; for

the world too, at large, and so love, Crystal Yehuwdiyth,

babe, I will end here; let you go babe, my love, to go and

to do what you got to do; also thank you for your time,

love, and energy too; also, for your cooperation. I love

you love; also, I will bless you too; thanks again, love,

for everything and for being MY LOVE and MY humble DOVE

too; so, love, keep the love coming; flowing to ME and for

ME too, POPS, LOVE MYSELF. I love you babe and take care.

Shalom, POPS, LOVE MYSELF, YAHWA, THE GOD OF LOVE,OF

INFINITY.

(Crystal Yehuwdiyth): thank you, POPS, for you and for

everything in general; I love you too tremendously; thanks,

once again, for letting me to play a part too. I love you

forevermore, for eternity. Take care and thanks again, for

coming through too, like always; shalom, shalom.

(POPS speaking): No problem, babe; also, I thank you for

your help, and for your sweet and kind words here; you are

welcome too love, my babe, Crystal Yehuwdiyth. Take care

and be good always; hang in there, babe, for I, POPS, LOVE

is here too, for <u>YOU</u> and for the rest of MY <u>CREW</u>. Shalom

again, POPS, LOVE MYSELF, THE GOD of LOVE, who is also real

humble as a dove too. LOL….

INTRODUCTION FOR HIS POEM CALLED:

("They that KEEP ME and MY LOVE will not LOSE ME")

Okay, shalom my very precious beloved love, Crystal

Yehuwdiyth, here's the deal, love, I am very, very proud of

you, love Crystal Yehuwdiyth, My sweet, sweet angel of

love, for letting and allowing ME, POPS, LOVE MYSELF,

YAHWA, to come on through, through you to say and to share

MY thoughts, lines and rhymes; also My poems with you; also

with the world out there and that is at large, just for

them to be able to hear ME; also to know that I AM their

God, Father and King too, that is absolutely real, just

like you and I; them too, and that I, POPS, LOVE MYSELF,

can actually speak, type and write too, just like I, POPS,

YAHWA, LOVE MYSELF, have bless them and you too, to do also; so, Love, Crystal, I'd like to say thank you very, very much for PLEASING ME and not TEASING ME; also for helping and for doing this with ME and for ME, POPS, LOVE MYSELF; along with ME, LOVE MYSELF, THE GOD of LOVE. And so, love, it is an absolute PLEASURE, my sweet, sweet TREASURE to come on through you, to present MY poem called, "THEY that KEEP ME and MY LOVE will not LOSE ME (MY LOVE that is); so world, I'd like to say this here, is absolutely apart of MY bid; bids too, that MY babe and love, Crystal Yehuwdiyth and I, is doing here, while we write, type and produce our books for you all to enjoy with an open heart, mind and spirit; soul to receive our very precious skills, talents, words , poems and lyrics of love with love, that is absolutely just like GOLD, but that is

worth much more than GOLD; but also, that is absolutely

good for every SOUL, and that's whether, they, or you are

YOUNG, or OLD, either way, our poems of GOLD that is good

for the SOULS is absolutely BEAUTIFUL, REFRESHING and BOLD;

so, get ready to get your heart filled with MY beautiful,

beautiful poem, rhymes and lines, that I am about to say

and DROP, just like this and NON-STOP too, but that will

absolutely make your eyes POP; your heart FILLED and

FULFILLED with MY LOVE; so MY love Crystal, and MY loves

out there here's My poem; it goes like this….

(Poem begins on the following page)

Poem title:

"<u>THEY</u> that <u>KEEP ME</u>, and <u>MY LOVE</u> will not lose <u>ME</u>"

Hey, hey, hey…. My sweet, sweet little <u>DOVES</u> and MY very

precious <u>LOVES</u>, here's, what I, POPS, LOVE MYSELF, YAHWA,

YHWH, got to say MY loves, is this, they that <u>KEEP ME</u> and

<u>MY LOVE</u> will not <u>LOSE ME</u>; nor <u>CONFUSE ME</u> with anyone else;

nor <u>DEFUSE ME</u>, <u>LOVE</u> that is, GOD ALMIGHTY, YAHWA, YHWH, out

of their lives; nor will they <u>ABUSE</u> ME, POPS that is; nor

will they let ME, POPS, LOVE that is, YAHWA, THE KING of

LOVE goes to <u>WASTE</u>; but that they will continue to <u>FUSE ME</u>,

LOVE that is; <u>MYSELF</u>, in their very precious lives every

time, every day and in every way and in anyway. For they

knows that LOVE MYSELF, YAHWA, is the <u>KEY</u> to everything and everything that is GOOD, SWEET and LOVING, and that's even

in the OVEN; in fact, a LOVE like this; or a LOVE like ME,

will forever be THERE; will not go ANYWHERE as long as

you're THERE and HERE for ME, too, I, POPS, LOVE MYSELF,

will never be missing in ACTION; nor in PROTECTION;

AFFECTION. For, I AM that LOVE that LOVE; that GOD that is

on MY job every TIME; for every MIND; especially for those

who are MINES, like this one here, Crystal Yehuwdiyth, who

is doing MY absolute bid, at this time; every time, I want

to say a LINE; a RHYME and to make ME, POPS, LOVE MYSELF,

SHINE, always coming through EVERY TIME she have; has ME,

GOD ALMIGHTY, LOVE MYSELF, her sweet and loving POPS in

MIND to DINE; so, you see loves; a LOVE like that will have

ME in her LINE; in her CORNER and in her QUARTER, simply,

because she doesn't seek to LOSE, ME, POPS LOVE MYSELF,

but to keep ME, very CLOSE and very NEAR, and that, to ME

is FAIR and real CLEAR. And that, to ME, lets ME know that

she's a DEAR that really CARES; also that, likes to SHARE,

and that, there, loves is pretty CLEAR, for if it wasn't

so, you all, out there, who is not FAIR to ME, wouldn't

HEAR ME, POPS, LOVE MYSELF, at all, if she and some of MY

others, love ones, who really CARES; who could really HEARS

ME speak and spit MY LINES didn't CARE, or CARE to HEAR ME

at all, but here's the proof that I, POPS, is making

MYSELF, CLEAR, that I AM HERE, THERE; also NEAR, just by

coming through MY love and love ones, who lets ME through

to let you all know that I AM their LOVE that will not seek

to LOSE them; nor to be FAR, but I AM that LOVE that will

always be <u>THERE</u>, for MY true <u>LOVE</u> ones that truly, truly

<u>CARES</u>; they are the <u>LOVES</u> and MY <u>LOVES</u> who seeks to <u>KEEP</u> ME

and <u>MY LOVE</u> within arm's reach; also within their hearts,

they are the ones that will not <u>LOSE</u> ME; nor MY <u>LOVE</u>, for

they are really and truly special to ME, above <u>ANY</u> and <u>MANY</u>

other materials; why do I say that? It is, because they are

absolutely, a <u>DEAR</u> to ME, that brings a whole lot of <u>CHEER</u>

and <u>LAUGHTER</u> to ME and for ME too; so, love; MY loves out

there, I'd like to say, to you all, that MY loves, who <u>KEEP</u>

<u>ME</u> and MY <u>LOVE</u> deep <u>DOWN INSIDE</u>, and that is <u>WISE</u>, and that

will <u>RISE, RISE, RISE</u> to MY occasions with <u>LOVE</u> in their

<u>HEARTS</u> and from the very <u>START</u> will never, never lose ME,

POPS, LOVE MYSELF; nor MY very precious <u>LOVE</u> for them. For

they are absolutely deserving of ME, POPS, always and all

of the time; they are the ones that are in <u>MIND</u> every time,

simply, because they have proven to ME, POPS, YAHWA, LOVE

MYSELF, through their <u>WORKS</u>, <u>WORDS</u> and <u>ACTIONS</u> without the

<u>DISTRACTION</u>, that they are the loves, who <u>WANTS ME</u>, <u>NEEDS</u>

<u>ME</u> and that will always seeks to <u>KEEP ME</u>, <u>LOVE ME</u> and not

<u>REFUSE ME</u>, or <u>ABUSE</u> me; nor <u>MISUSE ME</u>, but that will always

<u>KEEP ME</u> in their minds, hearts, spirits; also within their

souls, simply, because they know for sure, that I am <u>GOLD</u>;

also the <u>GOLD</u> for everyone; every <u>SOUL</u> that won't <u>FOLD</u>; nor

runs <u>COLD</u>, but that will continue to be <u>BRAVE</u> and <u>BOLD</u>;

also very <u>WARM</u>, <u>TENDER</u> and <u>SWEET</u> to all of MY very

precious loves and doves, that always seeks to <u>KEEP ME</u> and

<u>MY LOVE</u> within their inwards <u>PARTS</u> and <u>HEARTS</u>, and for

that, love Crystal; you all MY loves, I will say that, you

who are LOVE, will never, never LOSE ME, but see ME time

and time again; also will feel ME time and time again;

forever and eternally too. And so, loves, Crystal, Sarai,

Pearl and my boy Troy too, continue to be MY loves that are

willing to keep ME close and not far away; also that will

absolutely continue to KEEP ME, POPS, LOVE MYSELF, for you

all are MY GOLD and LOVES that I, POPS will always KEEP and

never wants to LOSE; so, remember that, Crystal; you all My

other loves, are MY LOVES who have showed to ME, POPS, LOVE

MYSELF, that you all wants and is willing to KEEP ME, POPS

and MY LOVE always; so shalom, I love you babe, Crystal, my

love; thank you for allowing ME, POPS, GOD ALMIGHTY, LOVE

MYSELF, to come on through, to do MY PART from the HEART;

also to show MY SKILLS with your FREEWILL; while I CHILL

and feels THRILL to do your and our WILL, without feeling

ILL; so now love, Crystal Yehuwdiyth, My sweet angel of

love, I , POPS, LOVE YAHWA will seek to CHILL ; before I do

love, Crystal, I'd like to thank you babe for everything;

also for allowing ME to say a word, or two to the world, to

let them know that MY LOVES, who seeks to KEEP ME and MY

LOVE; who will not LOSE ME, is the ONES that are doing MY

WILL with their FREEWILL with a THRILL and with a sparkle

in their eyes; so, loves, if you are that one, or love that

is doing so, then you will be the ones that will love ME,

POPS, LOVE MYSELF, too; so this is to let you all know

that, I, POPS, LOVE MYSELF, knows who truly and really

loves ME; of those who don't; so, as a result of that, you

all will absolutely be SAD, MAD and not GLAD, because I,

POPS, too, will not mine LOSING you all, who doesn't LOVE

ME; nor willing to KEEP ME and MY LOVE; I will simply turn

you over to HATE; so you all can continue to MATE; while it

will be LATE; too LATE for you to CONTEMPLATE; or to DEBATE

with ME, POPS, LOVE MYSELF. For I, LOVE MYSELF, POPS, THE

GOD OF LOVE; OF THE HEAVENS will take MY true loved ones,

who didn't want to LOSE ME, but to KEEP ME and MY LOVE;

shower them with LOVE always and throughout eternity; that

is why I say that MY LOVES who KEEPS ME and MY LOVE will

never LOSE ME (POPS, LOVE ALMIGHTY and GOD ALMIGHTY) at

all. And so, loves, this is something to think about,

before the FINAL HOUR and before you fully become SOUR. For

I AM the POWER of LOVE and the POWER; the LOVE that is from

up ABOVE with much, much LOVE for all, my love ones; not

just for one that is; so seek to be one of MY loves that is

willing to KEEP ME and MY LOVE, so you won't LOSE ME, POPS,

LOVE MYSELF, YAHWA, GOD ALMIGHTY, that is here speaking and

writing for MYSELF, along with My very precious Daughter,

Crystal Yehuwdiyth, MY helper and MY sweet angel of love

(ME), YAHWA; so give us thanksgiving and the love for doing

our PART and our WORK of ART to you all; for you all with

love. For without US who loves you all, you all wouldn't

know whose LOVE; or what's on our minds; nor on our plate.

So, shalom and take care. I love you all and thanks again,

babe Crystal and for that I will bless you for it. Shalom

again, this have and has been ME, POPS, LOVE MYSELF, YHWH,

YAHWA, THE GOD of LOVE; OF INFINITY and BEYOND; My typist

and daughter; love, Crystal Yehuwdiyth Yehowshabath

Yisrael, my angel of love; disciple of love, Martha; not

Martha Stewart. LOL..., LOL....

(Crystal Yehuwdiyth): Thanks Pops, MR. LOVE YAHWA, the GOD

of LOVE, for everything in general; also, for your time,

love, and support; also, for coming through like the way

you do. For I appreciates your poem here, for it well said

and well put together too, for it is very heartfelt, it

made my heart melt, just to hear you say what you said here

on your real wonderful work that you have done here, I am

truly, truly impress with it and with you too, also love;

thank you for expressing yourself to me and to the world

wide world, like you did with all honesty, fire and with a

genuine passion and love. For that there, LOVE, POPS have

reach out and touch me deep, deep down inside; it even made

me cry and shed a tear or two out of joy and a good feeling

of jubilee, and I have you to thank for it always. Pops,

LOVE YAHWA, I must say that you have laid your rhymes and

lines and words; lyrics real perfectly ; thank you for

letting it be known that we are your angel of love; your

loves that is deserving of your love; believe me, it is a

good thing to hear that; also to see you express that to

the world; believe me, Pops, LOVE YAHWA, I am glad to be an

angel of love; of yours, who has you on my team; also who

has your love too; believe me, Pops, I am glad to have you

in my life and I truly doesn't wants to lose you, or your

love also, for you and your love is very precious to me and

that it, you means a lot to me too; thanks for letting us,

me know of how you feel; felt. And trust me, you and your

love are worth keeping every time and in mind. Thanks for

being the love and the father; God and hero, too that is

here for me, us all and that is here cheering us, me on. I

love you love and keep up the good, good work always, for

your poems, rhymes and lines are absolutely delicious and

very precious and good and sweet to the bone; to my soul

too; so good luck and have fun in doing what that you are

doing and that you do have in mind always. For, it was, and

it is fun always working and typing with you. I love you

forever and eternally too. Shalom, Crystal Yehuwdiyth, your

angel of love that loves you dearly. LOL...

And so, now, Pops, LOVE, you can and comment if you like.

Would like to comment, although I know that you are busy,

but I don't mine, if you don't. LOL… it's up to you love

and I'll be quiet, so what do you say Dad? LOL…., LOL…

(POPS Talking): Okay, love, my love and beloved daughter,

Crystal Yehuwdiyth, here I am , Pops, LOVE MYSELF, the GOD

of LOVE, who is now here speaking for MYSELF, once again,

my friend and darling, Crystal Yehuwdiyth; here's what I,

POPS, LOVE MYSELF, YAHWA, YHWH, GOD ALMIGHTY, Your dad of

heaven and of old has to say to you, my love and very

precious daughter here Crystal, is this, you have done a

real wonderful job in responding to ME, POPS, LOVE MYSELF,

the GOD of LOVE, your old man and father, YHWH, YAHWA, and

that love, I do truly appreciates a great, great deal;

thanks for being for real in what you do; also in what you

say and means too. For I truly felt it and feel it too,

love, that it is filled with a whole lot of love too, babe,

your words babe, that I mean; believe Me, I, POPS, LOVE

MYSELF, is absolutely moved and touch too, by your very

precious comments that you have made to Me, POPS, your old

loving Dad and father; God too; for that I am well PLEASED

and at EASE with you; also I am truly thankful to you for

taking the time out to comment on MY work; works of ART

that is absolutely from My HEART from the very, very START.

So, love, Crystal Yehuwdiyth, my darling and my real sweet,

sweet angel of love, I'd like to say that I am really

impress with your works, words and with your actions too,

love; so thank you for the joy and for the fun love, that

you always bring with you love, for I, POPS, truly, truly

appreciates it; also it really do charges ME up every time

love; so keep up the good work going and the love for ME

growing, ok love, and I love you totally and tremendously;

eternally also. And so, love Crystal, I, POPS, LOVE MYSELF,

is about ready to leave and skedaddle, but before I do, I

would like to let you know, babe, that you have absolutely

made My day too; and not only that, but that you have

truly, truly impress ME too, in your addressing Me on My

works and skills too; for that I, POPS, LOVE MYSELF, YAHWA,

YHWH, is happy; will definitely bless you for that, real

abundantly too; so, you just watch and see, love Crystal,

what I do love, real, real soon; so enjoy you all's selves

babe, when you gets to my babe, Doretha's house later on,

for I, POPS, YAHWA and my babe Doretha will have a lot

going on for you all; also, it will be possible for you all

to stay too, and so, just relax and be on the lookout for a

couple of days off the streets loves, Crystal and Pearl,

for I, POPS, YAHWA, is working on it as we speak and also

is typing loves; so, be on the lookout for the call from

ME, POPS, LOVE MYSELF; from my babe Doretha real, real

soon; so don't be a buffoon loves and pass on that offer,

for the library will always be there; that opportunity will

not always be there; here for you all, ok love; so Crystal

and Pearl, be sure to be focus and to listen up for ME,

POPS, YAHWA, when I call to be on the ball without stalling

loves; so loves it's all up to you all loves, for I, POPS

and My daughter Doretha is already doing our parts, and so

get started on thinking on what you all will do, as far as

getting there before MY storm starts again, ok loves, I

love you all and have a bless day, for I, we will be

blessing you all altogether; so be happy and relax this

weekend; I love you loves; take care and do the right thing

loves, seek to make you all's way there real soon, even if

you all have to stroll there, okay loves, just so when we

call, you all will already be there on that end. My work is

already done loves; so now it's just a matter of you all

doing you all's part from the heart; so, TA, TA loves

Crystal and Peal, I love you all once again; be good and

have a good one loves; shalom. Good job babe, I just love

it, your words and works too. Shalom, Pops, LOVE MYSELF,

YAHWA, YHWH, THE GOD OF ALL HEAVENS, EARTH.

(Crystal):Praise you, LOVE, POPS, YAHWA, for your love,

time and concerns; also for coming through and for doing

what you do, which showing your love, power and skills that

is always absolutely real beautiful and amazing too, kudos

to you Pops, Dad, for your magic touch; touches, for truly

you have the Midas touch for real, for every time you touch

something it turns to gold and ends up being good for every

soul; good job, LOVE, I am really please and impress with

your works and thank you for being there for me, us all;

keep up the good work of love always; thanks for being our

hero, once again, I love you forever and eternally too,

take care LOVE, POPS, YAHWA. For truly you are amazing and

true for real and to me; for me too. Shalom, have a bless

day Pops. Love, Crystal Yehuwdiyth.

(POPS): Ok, babe, Crystal Yehuwdiyth, I am totally grateful

to you here babe, for what you have said here my love;

truly I, Pops, LOVE MYSELF, your old love and Dad of old,

is truly touch once again, by what you lay down on your

book and paper, as your lines and rhymes love; that's every

time babe; so thanks for being grateful and thankful to Me

and for Me, POPS, LOVE MYSELF, GOD ALMIGHTY, YAHWA; so babe

Crystal, my love quit being so, so comical love, I know

that you sometimes can't help yourself, but try, try babe

try. LOL...., for you are absolutely something else love; so

take care and have a bless day too; enjoy you all's selves;

me and babe, my love Sarai, you all's Emma will talk to you

all real, real soon, okay; so just bear with us love,

Crystal and Pearl, ok loves; shalom, I love you all, always

and forever; thanks again babe for your love and time; for

your cooperation too.

Shalom, POPS, ME, LOVE MYSELF, THE GOD OF LOVE.

Pops, preface and thoughts on his poem:

"My TRUMPTERS of LOVE is my WORKERS of LOVE"

Okay, shalom, my beloved love, Crystal Yehuwdiyth, this is

your POPS, LOVE MYSELF, that is here coming through you

love to come forth to bring forth MY real beautiful poem

here, that I, POPS, YAHWA, titled Myself, which is called

"MY TRUMPTERS of LOVE is MY WORKERS of LOVE; so, My love,

Crystal, I'd like to say that thank you, my love, for

having your old man and Dad of heaven; of the entire

universe to come on through to say MY piece and MY lines

and rhymes to you all; to the world at large, babe Crystal,

and so, here it goes; as I, POPS, YAHWA, YHWH, lays down

MY lines, rhymes and poem, I am POPS, LOVE MYSELF, YAHWA,

the GOD of LOVE; of INFINITY, that is here to say to you

all, the world at large that MY TRUMPETERS of LOVE is MY

WORKERS of LOVE, that is from UP ABOVE; that is FULL and

FILLED with LOVE; also, MY TRUMPTERS of LOVE, of MINE that

is, is a LOVE; the LOVES that are as humble as a DOVE; that

is THERE, HERE; also that is NEAR for ME and with ME, POPS,

LOVE MYSELF; that is SERVING ME and the whole WIDE WORLD at

LARGE, while I'm in CHARGE; for that MY LOVES out there,

you all that is in the world at large, has to give ME, POPS

and MY sweet, sweet angels and not the devils (want to be)

in hell, the LOVE and the RIGHTFUL RECOGNITION that they

needs and deserves, for with ME, POPS, LOVE MYSELF, they

are the ones that is working with ME and along with ME,

POPS, GOD ALMIGHTY, LOVE MYSELF, to help ME out and to help

make MY job and jobs a tad bit more easier; more; more

faster, although, I am the GOD of LOVE, who do all things

all by Myself; who can supersedes all BEINGS and THINGS,

but keep in mind that, I, too needs help too, to work the

world; to work the love for you all; to you all, for

without ME, POPS, the GREATEST LOVE ; the HIGHEST PARENT,

who is the very first WARNER; the very first TRUMPETER, you

all would end up in the DUMPSTER with NO love at all; so,

that is why I, POPS, LOVE MYSELF,YAHWA, says that MY

TRUMPETERS of LOVE is MY WORKERS of LOVE with MY love. And

so, loves, do you now see why, MY TRUMPETERS of LOVE, like

this one here, My lovely daughter Crystal Yehuwdiyth; My

other love ones, like My real sweet, sweet and loving wife

Sarai Nechawmaw and My sweet, sweet babe; love, Pearl

Abiygail too; also My beautiful boy and son, Troy

Mattithyah, deserves the love; the recognition too; so, I

hope you all do, because they are the ones, that are

absolutely and actually doing the work of love; MY work of

art that is real beautiful and amazing, which is MY very

sweet and precious; insightful bids, that none other of you

are actually doing; that's even when I, POPS, LOVE MYSELF,

COMPLAIN and experience PAIN , still , there's no other of

My love ones, who shows the LOVE, but MY true, true

TRUMPETERS of LOVE, who truly are MY WORKERS of LOVE, that

is working the work of love and the love to you all; for

you all, who doesn't answer MY CALLS; nor gets on the BALL

for ME, or for MY bids and NEEDS; also you all who are not

MY WORKERS of LOVE; nor MY TRUMPETERS of LOVE, you all will

see the end results; insults that you cause, by not willing

to do, or to help ME out; believe ME, POPS, LOVE MYSELF,

will definitely, let and make you all see that, it wasn't a

good idea to not deal with ME; not to help ME out, in

shouting out, that I, LOVE MYSELF and GOD ALMIGHTY,

although I AM GOD and the HIGHEST MAN above, that I still

need, LOVE, RESPECT and the HELP for I too got NEEDS;

FEELINGS too; so, MY dear loves out there in the world,

that is what I, POPS, LOVE MYSELF, expected to do; that I

finds out that you all are not doing for ME; it's simply

because you all are not MY TRUMPETERS of LOVE; nor MY

WORKERS of LOVE, who loves ME; nor the GAME; or the GAME of

LOVE, that would and will help you and I, to SOAR and FLY

high; while we, you and I, gets our work done by and

through warning the world of what's to come; of what will

happen to help them, you and all, to consider to change,

their evil and very wicked WAYS that's been there for DAYS;

that will definitely will not PAY their WAY out of HELL;

yes, believe ME, those WAYS of MY loves there, that are

absolutely REBELIOUS and real RIDICULIOUS, I am absolutely

not WELL with; nor WELL PLEASED with; I, POPS, will say

that, you all there, loves, who are on the OUT SKIRTS; that

is not NEAR ME, POPS, LOVE MYSELF, will have a DAY where

LOVE MYSELF, will have a DAY where you all will YELL,

SCREAM and SHOUT, but not for MY BIDS, but for MY LOVE that

you all will not have for a time, until ME and MINE, POPS

that is, LOVE, is done UNWIND; being just FINE and feeling

real DIVINE; SET and SHINE; also DINE with ME, POPS, MR.

LOVE MYSELF, who are there with ME and have been HERE and

THERE with ME, POPS, who is <u>LOVE</u> that is, because they love

ME; also, because they <u>CARE</u> for ME; also that wanted to

help <u>SPARE ME</u>, from a whole <u>LOAD</u> of work load through their

love for ME; for their work of love, and that there is

clearly letting you all, the world know that, they are the

loves who showed love to ME, by and in any way, shape,

form, or fashioned, are THE and MY TRUMPETERS of LOVE, that

is MY true WORKERS of LOVE, that cares about LOVE, ME,

MYSELF; also for you all too, who need to <u>REALIZE</u> and to

open your and you all's <u>EYES</u> to this truth, that I am the

GOD of LOVE, that has a whole lot of LOVE for you all; that

I am the <u>LOVE</u> that is here to help <u>SAVE</u> you all; so don't

<u>STALL</u> and stop the <u>STALLING</u> of being MY <u>TRUMPETERS of LOVE</u>,

and that would make you all the and MY WORKERS of LOVE, for

after all, I AM the HIGHEST of them ALL. In other words, I

AM the very first; also the HIGHEST TRUMPETER of LOVE; that

is with an absolute LOVE that is ABOVE; that is from up

ABOVE and that is here to give to you all nothing, but

LOVE, but one thing that is for sure, loves, is that MY

WORLD, MY LOVE and MY WORKERS of LOVE; MY TRUMPETERS with

LOVE, will supersede all of you, who doesn't think that I

AM the GOD, who is ALMIGHTY, and that I AM able and

capable; stable enough to do all of those; these things all

by MYSELF; that does; needs and also that is deserving of

the helping HANDS, but as it STANDS ; as WE and I, ME and

MY sweet daughter of LOVE, ME of course, comes to an end

here, I will say that, she is one of MY TRUMPETERS of LOVE;

so that makes her, one of MY WORKERS of LOVE also; so, I

will say thank you love, Crystal Yehuwdiyth, for your help,

strength, courage and perseverance; also for your

willingness; for your love for ME, POPS, LOVE MYSELF; for

that, love, I am well, well PLEASE; at EASE with you love,

for allowing ME, POPS, LOVE MYSELF, to come on through to

say MY piece to you and the world at large; while I bring

forth MY poem, the way I see FIT, and that to ME, love, is

a HIT for ME, and for YOU too; what I mean, is this love,

our book "THE RHYMESTER of LOVE is MY PRIESTESS with LOVE",

will definitely soar loves, Crystal and Pearl; believe Me,

babe, it will and I sure will make it happen for you and I;

us all, who are writing, creating and producing this very

special book here with love; so, babe, my love Crystal and

Pearl too, just watch and see, that you all's POPS, LOVE

MYSELF, at; indeed, I will work to see that the world at

large sees and recognizes that, we are the WORKERS of LOVE,

who are the LOVES from <u>ABOVE</u>; also the TRUMPETERS of LOVE,

who truly loves them all; that have done our <u>ALL</u> to help

out <u>ALL</u>, our loves before the <u>FALL</u> that is <u>COMING</u>, and that

we will truly escape, because of our LOVE for all, that we

have <u>DISPLAYED</u> and <u>REPLAYED</u>, over and over without a <u>DELAY</u>;

so, love, I love you and all, my loves; so, babe Crystal,

take care and remember that, I will absolutely bless you

for your hard work; also for the love for ME, POPS; so,

shalom, babe and thanks again for keeping your word and

goodnight; don't let the bed bugs bite.(LOL!) Thanks babe

and I love you eternally and everlastingly.

This is POPS;LOVE MYSELF YAHWA,THE GOD of LOVE;OF INFINITY.

(Crystal Yehuwdiyth): Thank you, POPS, LOVE for everything

in general; also, thanks for your time, energy, love, and

support; also, for coming through too; I love you very,

very much and forever; eternally too. And you, LOVE is

quite…. quite welcome; shalom and take care; goodnight too.

(POPS): Oh, thank you my babe, Crystal Yehuwdiyth, for I

truly, truly appreciates you for your time and patience

too; also for hanging in there to see ME, POPS, through and

through MY poems of love; that's with love, for and to you

to all my loves out there in the world, and for that, love

Crystal, you are appreciated and you are quite, quite

welcome indeed. Shalom love and take care. POPS, LOVE

MYSELF. I love you forever and eternally too.

(Crystal Yehuwdiyth): Praise you, LOVE, praise you love!!!

For truly you are deserving of it all. Shalom, Crystal

Yehuwdiyth, your angel of love; your trumpeter of love

always. LOL…

(POPS speaking):No problem, babe, no problem, for I Pops,

YAHWA, truly appreciates that there; that line there very,

very much; so, kudos to you too, babe; once again, as I end

for sure, I'd like to say I love you eternally;

forevermore. LOL…, it's just a joy love working with you,

love, for you are a lot of fun, thank God, ME that it's not

in the sun. LOL… shalom, shalom, babe, my angel of love; of

course, signing off, and the boss of course…Ha! Ha! Ha! Ha!

My preface and thoughts on:

(my Poems coming forth)

Hi and shalom, my loves and family, of course this I,

Crystal Yehuwdiyth Yehowshabath Yisrael, that is here

introducing myself, simply to let you all know that now

that my Heavenly and God, YAHWA, YHWH, THE GOD OF LOVE, is

done rapping and spitting his real marvelous and absolutely

amazing lines and rhymes on every lines, I would like to

let you know that now it is my time too, spit and to lit

every line that I can, but don't get it twisted, I can

never beat the best, although I learned from the rest, but

it is an absolute fact jack, that I can't and will never be

able to catch up; or to match up with the most High, who is

the best out of all the rest. LOL..., LOL.... Well, anyway,

loves, what I would like to mention to you all, is this, my

and our Heavenly Father held his sit, grounds every, every

round and even his crown; that is without a single frown.

And so, do you know what that means? Well, it means that he

cannot be defeated, for he is complete; completely

unbeatable, hands down; or hands up, He, YAHWA, THE GOD OF

LOVE, MR. LOVE HIMSELF, is an all-around type of guy, God

and king. In a nutshell, He rules and run everything, just

like the king that he is and will forever be. LOL...., Well,

loves, enough said here. LOL... As a matter of fact, I wanted

to let you all know; or to be aware of this fact here, that

on the following page and pages to come down the line; or

down the pipeline, will be my poems that will be on display

from my mind and from my lips, putting them in gear to

shine bright; so, be on look out the <u>six poems</u> that I have

and will be bringing forth with an opened mind; also, with

a humbling spirit; further, with a happy heart. At the end

of the day, my goal is to uplift all with our all, my poems

and with my Heavenly Father's poems as well with love; so,

loves, let's do this for love's sake and for our sake as

well. LOL… So, I, WE love you all; here they are my poems

of love that is, with love. Shalom, shalom; praise LOVE,

The GOD; the FAMILY OF LOVE always; forevermore from the

core with gladness and not in distress. LOL….

Poem title:

"THOU shall NOT KILL"

THOU shall not KILL,

Because LOVE is what should THRILLS us.

Also, because LOVE; LIFE is what we NEED and to BRED

Simply, because, LOVE is the ONE that gives to us the good

feeling; also, that gave to you and me, the FREEWILL

To do his Divine WILL, and not to KILL!

Furthermore,

THOU shall not KILL,

Because LOVE came about to UPLIFT

You and I; to keep us ALIVE and to make us FLY HIGH

Way ABOVE the HATE, the NEGATIVITY, and the EVIL thoughts

That will lead you to KILL.

And so, loves, just keep in <u>MIND</u>, that it is not <u>FINE</u> at

all to <u>KILL</u>, but that, is absolutely <u>DIVINE</u> to have <u>LOVE</u> in

your <u>MIND</u>; also, as your <u>FORCE</u> and <u>BACKBONE</u> in your <u>SPINE</u>,

to be able to <u>CHILL</u>; to keep away the <u>ILL WILL</u> that would,

or that will lead to you and me, or us to <u>KILL</u>.

And, again I say that,

<u>THOU</u> shall not <u>KILL</u>.

For this is not our GOD (YHWH'S) given

<u>SKILL</u>; Nor his <u>WILL</u>.

And so, loves, once again,

Let us, you, and me, think about this,

Just so, we won't <u>MISS</u>; or <u>DISMISS</u> the most important

thing, which is to love first, LOVE Himself; as well, his

very precious commandments; then to turn away from your; or

our WAYS, that's been there for DAYS. In fact,

Just so, you, we, or I, won't go on a SPREE, or on a

STREET; PATH that will lead us to KILL.

For after all,

One of His LAWS

Was and is, THOU shall not KILL.

For to do so, which is to KILL, would just lead

You and me or us into a MESS that we wouldn't,

Or couldn't be able to DASH from; nor to CAST.

And, I say that, because

To take a LIFE, or to DEPRIVE a LIFE,

A LOVE, a PERSON; or a BEING, or any LIVING THING from

LIVING, would be WRONG, a DISGRACE and something DOWNGRADED

that would not help uplift your soul; or our souls,

furthermore, it would be something that would not put a

smile on Love's <u>FACE</u>; nor would it be <u>SOMETHING</u> that He,

YAHWA, YHWH, would <u>EMBRACE</u> with a good <u>FACE</u>.

So, loves, just remember that,

GOD, YAHWA, LOVE Himself; ALMIGHTY,

Is a <u>LOVE</u> that is a <u>THRILLER</u>, and not a <u>KILLER</u>!!

For, this is not his way in the very first place.

And, I say this and that,

Because He,(LOVE that is)

Is <u>LIFE</u> and <u>LIFE</u>, is what He has and have given to us,

To enjoy and to experience with <u>JOY</u> and not with the <u>GRIEF</u>

and the <u>STRIFE</u>; so, be <u>NICE</u> and don't even think <u>TWICE</u>, for

this is my <u>ADVICE</u> to you all, about <u>LOVE</u>; which is to let

LOVE takes it COURSE and to be the BOSS; also, the SPICE

for our and your LIFE.

And so, as I close, I will say that don't KILL and just

CHILL OUT, out of the phase to KILL. For the COMMANDMENT of

LOVE was and is to LOVE one another; also, what was given

to us was and is, "THOU shall not KILL". (Exodus 20: 12)

<u>My thoughts on the introduction of my Pops coming forth:</u>

And now that, I am done presenting my poem called, "Thou shall not kill", to you all, I'd like to let you all know that, I am about to let my Heavenly Father and God, YHWH-YAHWA, MR. LOVE Himself, our Creator and Savior to come forth and to speak; also, to share his thoughts with me, through me and to you all, if he chooses to do so; so, as my and our Heavenly Father, step forth to drop down his lines and very precious rhymes, I'd like to say that, it is a pleasure to let him, YAHWA, YHWH, MR. LOVE HIMSELF, to come on through to shine and to do and say his thing and his part from the heart; so, LOVE, POPS, YHWH, YAHWA, come and say your part; while I stay quiet; so, LOVE, POPS,

YAHWA, I love you and you take the floor and it's all

yours. LOL….

MY POPS, YAHWA'S THOUGHTS ON

"THOU SHALL NOT KILL":

Okay shalom, my beloved daughter, Crystal Yehuwdiyth,

this is I, POPS, LOVE MYSELF, YAHWA, YHWH, THE GOD OF LOVE,

THE HOLYSPIRIT, that is here speaking with you; also for

MYSELF, love and don't go thinking that it is someone else,

that is here with you, or that is sitting within you,

because love, Crystal Yehuwdiyth, my beloved love and babe,

I heard you invited me in to join in on the fun too, while

we are not in the sun; or under the sun, but, anyway, I do

appreciate you and also do appreciate the fact, that you

love, my babe, Crystal that you hadn't, or haven't

forgotten Me, POPS, LOVE MYSELF; for that I am well, well

and very, very pleased too; thank you for doing that for

me, love; also I thank you too, for taking the time out to

do this for me and with me too; also for having me, POPS,

LOVE MYSELF, in mind at this time; believe me, every time

you do this, that truly make Me, POPS, that is, feels real,

real good deep down inside; that there love, Crystal is

truly, truly wise in my eyes love; also, I wanted to take

the time out to say thank you for writing this real, real

beautiful, beautiful and real amazing poem here, that have

absolutely blow my mind at this here time; also, my love

Crystal, I, POPS, LOVE MYSELF, YAHWA, would like to say

that I appreciate the fact that you have tried to call us

and to get in touch with us; that there, I truly, truly

appreciate and appreciated; for that I, POPS, LOVE YAHWA,

says kudos to you love; hoping to hear from you and you all

real, real soon; I hope that it's not after a full moon,

Loll… just being comical babe, my love Crystal, but anyway,

love, you have absolutely done a real good, good job in

doing this; also in presenting and in putting this poem

together my love Crystal Yehuwdiyth; so, keep up the good,

good work GOING and FLOWING; also SHOWING too, love for it

is absolutely, important to do so, for it will come a time,

where I, POPS, LOVE MYSELF, YAHWA, YHWH, will not be

allowing more, or no writing to be continued on, when it is

not its season, because I am getting ready loves, Crystal

Yehuwdiyth; Pearl Abiygayil, MY angels of love, to shut

down a whole lot of operations real, real soon loves; so,

that is why I am telling you all this; also, it is because

I need and want you all to work real, real hard and soon

too, on you all's books and skills that I, POPS have given

to you all, on and at an appoint time frame, that is

appropriate to Me, LOVE MYSELF, THE GOD OF LOVE, who is THE

HOLYSPIRT and the GOD of the UNIVERSE; of THE ENTIRE

PLANETS and GALAXIES. So, love Crystal, my love and babe,

seek to work real, real hard to get this book of yours and

of ours to be completed real, real soon, because I, Pops,

YAHWA, wants it to be put out there sometime soon, ok love,

(Crystal):Ok, Pops, I understand; also I hear you clearly;

thanks for saying that love, for I appreciate it too;

thanks for the encouragement; for your complements too, for

that means a lot to me , just to hear you say that and does

that, show the love and the support too, that is never

short; so, I love you, LOVE, POPS too, very, very much and eternally too. LOVE YAHWA, POPS, you are quite welcome too.

(POPS): Oh, my love and babe, Crystal Yehuwdiyth, I definitely would like to say thank you for your real sweet and kind words; I appreciate the fact, that you have taken the time out to respond back to Me, POPS, YAHWA; not only that, but that you have taken the time out to introduce ME, POPS, LOVE YAHWA, YHWH, to the world at large; for that I am totally grateful and thankful to you love, Crystal Yehuwdiyth; that there, truly, truly means a lot to Me, POPS, YAHWA, Myself, and so, love, before I skedaddle I would like to say that I haven't forgotten you all at all, loves; if anything, I will be doing something for you all, Pearl and Crystal, real, real soon; believe me, babe, I am not lying; nor just telling a tale either; I, POPS, LOVE MYSELF, says that, to say, that I will be taking over the whole matter here, concerning you all my loves ,Crystal and Pearl Abiygayil; it won't be left off, to them, meaning to my children, that's seeking to do and implement their own dealing and will, for they are seeking to do what they wants, but, I, POPS, LOVE YAHWA, THE GOD OF LOVE, is not going to stand by; nor sit with them and go along with their plans, for I, POPS, LOVE MYSELF, totally sees all that they got in their hands; I, POPS, LOVE MYSELF, THE KING OF LOVE, is saying this, because I want to let you all know that, I am the one that will be making things to happen; also that will be taking ACTIONS; that will be causing the REACTIONS that you will be getting from you all love ones, that will be around; around you all, that is

here at the Camillus house; believe Me, I am that <u>MAN</u> and

<u>GOD</u> of the <u>HIGHEST</u>; <u>FATHER</u> too, that will be making the

miracle; miracles for you all, loves, Crystal and Pearl

too, you all just watch and see, what will happen real,

real soon, when you all hear my daughter and I, MR. LOVE

calls you all in for the surprising results; don't be

surprise love, Crystal and Pearl, For I, POPS, LOVE MYSELF,

the GOD of LOVE, the HOLYSPIRIT, is already unfolding to

you all, how it will go down and of what will happen too,

for I , POPS, YAHWA, will see that all things workouts in

you all's favor, just like I, POPS, LOVE MYSELF, intends;

indented it to happen; it will loves, for I have the last

say so; the last words too; on top of that, the last action

and movement too; so thanks you for thanking Me in and for

every chance you get to; also for letting it be known too,

ahead of time, that it will be Me, POPS, YAHWA, YHWH, THE

GOD OF LOVE, that will be making all that will happen,

happen, by bringing it to their attention ahead of time

with some great amount of faith in Me, POPS, YAHWA, that

is; that I truly appreciates you all for; so be ready and

get set to take off, loves of the mat that is, love, for

the time is near; also is real, real close too; so loves

when it do and does happen don't forget to mention it to

them, my staffs and to my children them too, who somewhat

thinks and believes that it will not happen for you two, or

that it can't happen at all. For I will absolutely show

them whose <u>BOSS</u> of <u>COURSE</u>; believes me babes, I will; so, hold on to you all's socks and skirts too. Loll... And so,

loves, Crystal and Pearl, I, POPS, LOVE MYSELF, will be

closing out right now, but never, never my love, for I love

you all a great, great deal, forever and eternally too; so

love keep the love FLOWING and GOING for me and to me, too;

for I will forever do that for you all; so stay STRONG and

don't go WRONG and HANG ON, for I, POPS, LOVE MYSELF,

YAHWA, YHWH, The GOD of LOVE, is on my WAY to save the DAY

and to make a WAY love and loves; so shalom, babe Crystal,

and remember that I will absolutely bless you for your

time, energy and for your love and cooperation too; for

your willingness to allow Me to speak and share MY thoughts

with you; while, at the same time with the world also; at

large all at the same time, because the world is actually

seeing what I am saying here; so love I, POPS, LOVE YAHWA,

will say shalom and take care and continue love to keep ME,

in MIND always with something DIVINE every time; continue

to SHINE love just like you are doing; so look for brighter

and better days real, real soon loves. I love you all babes

and thanks again Crissy, for you have done a job well done

with love for me and to Me, POPS, too. Shalom again;

remember that love every poem here is a gold mine for the

souls and spirits that is out there; believe me, it will

absolutely help them to not KILL and to follow MY

COMMANDMENTS, for I and you, with your help we will see to

it; so, thanks again, for the work and the art of love from

the heart. Shalom, POPS, YAHWA, YHWH, THE GOD OF LOVE; OF

THE ENTIRE UNIVERSE.

(Crystal): Thank you, Pops, LOVE YAHWA, for your time,

energy and for your love and support too; also, for coming

through like you do and did too, for I truly appreciates it

love; so Pops, take care; also remember that I love you

always and eternally too; good, good job on what you have

said here and for letting me know of this and these

wonderful news too, for that is absolutely very, very

thoughtful of you to do and to say; also to share with me

too. I am so, so elated to know that you're the top man and

God in charge; also, that is large and the boss too; thank

you again for everything in general. Shalom, love and

Mizpah.

(Pops): Thank you, my babe and love Crystal, for all that

you have said here is absolutely sweet and touching too;

so, I appreciate it all; take care again and you are quite...

quite welcome too; so, love you again; shalom, POPS, LOVE

MYSELF, THE GOD OF LOVE, YAHWA.

The Preface for my poem:

(THY SHALL HONOR THY MOTHER AND FATHER)

Shalom loves and praise LOVE YAHWA- YHWH, who is the GOD of

LOVE, with love for his very precious love; as well, for

his gift of life with a delight. And so, here's my poem

called "Thou shall honor thy mother and father with love.

"And it goes a little something like this….

Poem title:

"<u>THOU shall HONOR thy MOTHER and FATHER with LOVE</u>"

THOU shall HONOR Thy MOTHER and FATHER (of HEAVEN), First,

before any <u>OTHER</u>, <u>BROTHERS</u> and <u>SISTERS</u>, our Earthly <u>MOTHER</u>

and <u>FATHER</u>; or any <u>OTHER</u>.

And why do I say that?

It is, because without them, our very precious and highest

parents, our MOTHER and FATHER of Heaven, who is our

highest LOVE, Mr., and Mrs. LOVE themselves, YHWH Yisrael,

there, wouldn't be anyone; nor any other.

Again, I say that,

THOU shall HONOR thy MOTHER and FATHER (of Heaven) with

<u>LOVE</u>; also, with the real <u>SWEET THINGS</u> of <u>HEAVEN</u>, that

doesn't possess anything, DIRTY, FILTHY, or JUST anything;

nor LEAVEN: Meaning a LEAVEN that is not of HEAVEN; you all

will truly see, what HEAVEN, our MOTHER and FATHER of the

Highest truly possesses within their MINDS, HEARTS,

SPIRITS; even within their SOULS without a LIMIT; with the

RICH things of LIFE that is filled with lots of MERITS, and

not with the things that will cause their DEMISE; or that

will cause them to be DEPRIVED.

And so, with that, keep that in mind; further, make sure

that there is MEMORIZED._LOL... For I left no room for anyone

to be SURPRISE.LOL...

Moreover, I say that,

THOU shall HONOR thy MOTHER and FATHER (of Heaven) with LOVE, because <u>LOVE</u> is what they have and has given to us; that's from day one.

In addition to that, I say again, THOU shall HONOR thy MOTHER and FATHER (of Heaven) with LOVE, because without them, or their LOVE, we wouldn't know how to <u>LOVE</u>; nor how to let it <u>SHOW</u>, or to <u>FLOW</u>; or even how to let it and to make it <u>GROW</u> and to <u>GLOW</u> above; or <u>BELOW</u>.

And so, loves, with that being said, I'd like to say that, that alone lets you and I, know that, that <u>HONOR</u> here, has to be given, simply because they (Our MOTHER and FATHER of HEAVEN) truly, truly deserves it; also, because they gives it to us all with their <u>ALL</u>; that's whether we are sitting down, or standing TALL, all they do, is let the love FLOW

and to FALL (upon us that is) and to cover us ALL, short or

tall, LOVE is what our MOTHER and FATHER of Heaven has

given to us all; so, let us remember to HONOR them with

LOVE; thanksgiving galore always and forevermore, for they

are absolutely SOMETHING and a SUPERIOR BEING; QUEEN and

KING that is very, very deserving of our RESPECT; of our

ADMIRATION; as well, that is to be eternally ADORED.

On top of that,

I say HONOR thy MOTHER and FATHER (of Heaven) with LOVE

because they came; have come time and time again; over and

over again, to help DELIVER us, COMFORT us; also to

REPLENISH us with their TIME, ENERGY, PATIENCE, COMPASSION

and with their absolute; <u>PURE</u> and <u>SURE LOVE</u>, just to keep

us <u>ABOVE</u> and not in <u>DESPAIR</u>; or in a <u>STATE</u> of being

<u>LOVELESS</u>; and that to me, is a <u>PLUS</u> and real <u>JUST</u>.

And, believe me, loves, it is not a <u>BUST</u>, but a <u>PLUS</u> and a

<u>MUST</u>, also a real TRUE <u>LOVE</u> and not <u>LUST</u>.

And, that there, truly makes me feels real special; also is

making me <u>BLUSH</u>; it is simply, because they are a <u>PLUS</u> that

is in my life, to keep me all <u>SENSIBLE</u>, <u>MUSHY</u> and <u>SWEET</u>

deep down in <u>INSIDE</u> and <u>OUT</u>; all ABOUT; that there, I don't

<u>DOUBT</u>; nor will <u>DOUBT</u>, for they have <u>REPLAYED</u> and

<u>DISPLAYED</u>, their <u>LOVE</u> with dignity in the <u>NORTH</u>, the <u>SOUTH</u>,

the <u>WEST</u> and even in the <u>EAST</u> with true, true <u>PEACE</u> that

was and that is absolutely <u>SWEET</u>, on the <u>BEAT</u>; also

<u>WHOLESOME</u> and <u>COMPLETE</u>.

And so, for that reason loves and more, I will say that

THOU shall (should) HONOR thy MOTHER and FATHER (of HEAVEN)

with nothing ELSE, or with nothing LESS, but with true,

true and with pure, pure LOVE always; forevermore.

More so, I say THOU shall (should) HONOR thy MOTHER and

FATHER (of HEAVEN), first; also, the earthly ones too,

meaning our earthly mother and father of earth, second in

line, and not above, or over the ones of HEAVEN, who are

our very FIRST and HIGHEST love, who help to quench our

THIRST for LOVE with their LOVE successfully and without a

BUST, or a DIGUST.

And so, loves, to me, Crystal Yehuwdiyth, who is an angel

of love; of the very, very first family and household of

heaven, is absolutely thrilled; also finds it to be a PLUS

and real JUST.

Overall and above all, I will say that, THOU shall (should)

HONOR thy MOTHER and FATHER (of Heaven), Mr. and Mrs. LOVE

YAHWA YISRAEL, because they are our AIR that we NEED;

BREATHE; also they are the LOVE that we feel deep down

INSIDE and WORLDWIDE; furthermore, they are the LIGHT that

we SEE with a DELIGHT, that gives to us SIGHT and INSIGHTS,

that is real TIGHT, RIGHT and DYNAMITE, and not only that,

but THOU shall (should) HONOR thy (your) MOTHER and FATHER

of Heaven, because they are absolutely the MAIN PART, the

GOLD HEART and the SWEETHEARTS that keeps us TOGETHER and

not APART; also that is working real hard and round the

CLOCK, to equip us and to STOCK us up; to keep us AFLOAT

and GOOD with all the divine STUFF and PARTS

(Of themselves) that is good, right and a delight, like

their minds, hearts, bodies, souls, and spirit too, that is

absolutely FULL of LOVE and not of the seeds of HATE that

is TART; or that is CONTAMINATED. In a nutshell, they, our

MOTHER and FATHER of HEAVEN, are the MAIN FRAME, MAIN

SYSTEM; the MAIN and ULTIMATE essence; the SPIRIT of LOVE;

for LOVE, for all of our hearts; also, so we can be able to

MAINTAIN and SUSTAIN the WRATH of HATE; also, so we can be

able to CONTAIN their divine SEEDS of LOVE with LOVE, and

to BE and to REMAIN who we are, and are to be with GLEE and

with JUBILLEE.

For, after all, this is what our MOTHER and FATHER of

HEAVEN wanted for us; also is fighting for, and is rooting

for, every time they reminds us through their divine

COMMANDMENTS and LAWS, STATUES and JUDGEMENTS, like the one

that says, if you LOVE ME (Him, them) KEEP MY (their)

COMMANDMENTS; also LOVE thy NEIGHBOR as you LOVE yourself;

furthermore, with the other law that says LOVE one another.

I love you all; to add to that, as I gets ready to close

out, I'd like to say, always remember to HONOR thy MOTHER

and FATHER of HEAVEN always and forever.

In a nutshell, as I officially close out, I would like to

say to you all that, THOU shall (should) HONOR thy MOTHER

and FATHER (of HEAVEN),

because they are TRUE; also, it's the RIGHT THING to DO;

further, it is because we are absolutely here because of

them; their love, also, it is, because they truly CARED;

CARES ; moreover, because they are FAIR, and not only,

because of that, but it is, because they truly deserves the

HONOR, the BANNER, the CROWN and the TITLE, simply because

they are the GREATEST and the BRAVEST ; the most LOVEABLE

parents, mother and father of them all; of Heaven that is

very, very SIGNIFICANT and VITAL; that's whether it above;

or below, and I say that because they are entitled to be

HONORED and RESPECTED in all ASPECT, that's simply because

, they are the MOST qualify; credible and trustworthy and

worthy to be trusted for their greatness, goodness,

GENEROSITY and for their BOUNTIFUL LOVE that is absolutely

VERIFIIABLE, WHOLESOME and DENSOME; AWESOME ; also that is

INCONTESTIBLE, by any other, mother, or father of earth; or

by any significant other.

And I say so, because they are the TRUE and the LIVING

Mother and Father of HEAVEN; of all LIVING, that is

absolutely LOVING, FORGIVING and that showed; shared their

LOVE for and to us, everyone that is ALIVE and LIVING, and

that there, is with all their hearts, minds, bodies, souls

and with their spirits and love that goes on and on;

relentlessly for me and for the whole wide. And so, for

that, let us HONOR thy MOTHER and FATHER of HEAVEN with a

constant LOVE and throughout eternity with jubilee

eternally.   Praise LOVE YAHWA, the GOD of LOVE.

(EPHESIAN 6:2, MATTHEW 19:19 and EXODUS 20:12)

POPS, YAHWA'S thoughts on:

"THOU shall HONOR Thy MOTHER and FATHER"

And now that, I am done presenting my poem, called "Thou shall honor thy mother and father", I would like to let you all know that my Heavenly Father, YHWH, YAHWA, MR. LOVE Himself, GOD ALMIGHTY, THE HOLYSPIRT, will be speaking for his self, just so he can elaborate on this here poem of mine, while he drops his lines and rhymes for us and right before us, just so, we can know what's on his mind at this here time; so, LOVE, POPS, YAHWA, YHWH, come on through and to spit and to say you line and what's on your mind at this time; I will be quiet, but before I do, I'd like to say that, I love you tremendously and eternally; also, good morning and have a bless and blissful day, and thanks for

wanting to come through for me and to say your very

precious piece at this time about my poem here; a whole lot

more, to let me, us know of what you have to say. And so,

LOVE, POPS, here's the floor and it's all yours to do your

thing. LOL…., LOL….; shalom.

(POPS speaking):Ok, my love and my beloved daughter,

Crystal Yehuwdiyth, this is your and you all's POPS, LOVE

MYSELF, YHWH, YAHWA, GOD ALMIGHTY, THE SPIRIT OF LOVE, and

the GOD OF LOVE, that is here speaking for Myself, just to

let you and you all know that I am well, well pleased with

you love; and that I am well, well pleased indeed with my

very precious daughter here, Crystal Yehuwdiyth, for taking

the time out to invite ME, POPS, LOVE MYSELF, to speak and

to say my piece here, to you all and to her; and that

there, is very sweet and very loving of her to do, just for

Me and just to definitely please ME, POPS, YAHWA, LOVE

MYSELF, who is THE GOD OF LOVE; OF THE ENTIRE UNIVERSE;

believe me, loves, I am definitely is well please and at

ease with her for her work that she is doing for Me and

with Me, POPS, LOVE MYSELF, just to keep you all in the

know too, I am working with her; along with her, side by

side, just to help open you all's eyes to this reality and

fact, that you all are to absolutely HONOR ME, POPS, LOVE

MYSELF, and also to HONOR, you all's heavenly MOM, MOTHER,

my daughter, wife and love, SARAI NECHAWMAW YISRAEL, for

she is the MOTHER of ALL, ALL LIVING, just like I AM the

FATHER of ALL, ALL LIVING, and that is here absolutely

giving to you all, the whole truth and nothing, but the

whole truth, that you all the world, are to be well aware

of, for this is a truth that's been HIDDEN and FORBIDDEN

for some time now, by MY enemies, who didn't want you all

to know of the truth, that there is and that there was a

real woman that existed with ME, POPS, LOVE MYSELF, YAHWA,

from that very, very beginning, right along with ME, GOD

ALMIGHTY, who created and made the heavens and the earth;

also of all the other things that was and is in it; are

found upon the earth; also within all of the other galaxies

and planets that I created and formed with MY own bare

hands; so, I, POPS, LOVE MYSELF, YAHWA, YHWH, THE GOD OF

LOVE, says this, to say that , none of you all where there

with ME, but my very precious wife Sarai, first, my very

first and only companion at that time, is the one that you

all are to be honoring, just like ME, POPS, YAHWA, YHWH,

LOVE MYSELF; also under ME, POPS, MR. LOVE MYSELF; anyway,

love, Crystal Yehuwdiyth and my loves, out there, I am that

GOD, MAN and FATHER, that you all are to be honoring with

much, much love always; forevermore; that I truly, truly am

serious about; trust me, loves; my love, Crystal, I will

see to it that, the world comes forth and honor ME and my

darling and lovely wife Sarai, who is putting in a whole

lot of work of love with ME, POPS, HER MAN, LOVE MYSELF,

and for ME too; that there the whole world will not miss

from hearing from Me, of course about her great, great

works that she have; has performed with Me, for Me and

along with Me, POPS, LOVE MYSELF, who is absolutely the GOD

OF LOVE, just to show and to prove her love for ME, POPS,

YAHWA, YHWH, and also, to you all, out there in the world,

who have; has totally forgotten of ME, POPS, YAHWA, YHWH,

and of her (Sarai) MY darling wife and love; mate too, who

is you all's mother and love too, but I got a trick for you

all who doesn't and who refuses to acknowledge that, I AM

to be honored; so do her too, for she have and has been

there and here too, for all of you; even for you all who

have ran and run from her (Sarai, you all's mother of

heaven); believe Me, I will see to it, that you all pay the

price, for neglecting her; also for neglecting Me, POPS,

LOVE MYSELF, you all's DAD of HEAVEN; POPS, LOVE MYSELF,

who is the FATHER of the entire UNIVERSE. For I see, it is

only a few that is recognizing that we are to be HONORED

very much so with a whole lot of love; that there is

absolutely ridiculous and outrageous , for it to be that

way, but all of that will absolutely change real, real

soon, cause I will see to it, that she gets her rightful

recognition, right along with MY others, like this one too,

who is Crystal Yehuwdiyth; right along with MY other love

ones, like my lovely daughter Pearl Abiygayil and My son,

Troy Mattithyah Yisrael, who have acknowledge that I am

real, alive; also living; also that is here taking care of

MY needs and seeds too; for that I will definitely please

them, put them at ease; also will make them happy too;

right along with fulfilling their needs too, that I will

absolutely make and let become priority to Me POPS, YAHWA,

LOVE MYSELF, and for Me too, for they have been there for

me too; and that I haven't forgotten; nor will ignore, for

they have made me smile for a while; while, at the same

time made Me, POPS, to have experience some real, real

beautiful days, when and while they plays their part and

parts from the heart with an absolute love that is true and

very sincere; believe me, that there is absolutely

refreshing and breathtaking and not disgusting, but ,

anyway, I will be honoring they them too, for their very

precious work; works too, that is and was of love exactly;

so, loves, my loves out there, you who doesn't seeks to

please ME, POPS, LOVE MYSELF, at all; also who doesn't

wanted to praise ME, honor ME and my love, Sarai, you all's

mom of heaven over you all's earth mom and dad, will

absolutely and definitely be sorry for real; will also

have something to worry about, for I, POPS, LOVE MYSELF, do

not accepts any foolishness like that at all; I will

absolutely seeks to change that, simply because she and I,

POPS, LOVE MYSELF; OURSELVES, is absolutely deserving of

that, the recognition; the honor of course, for we: meaning

ME and her have absolutely work; worked very, very hard to

help you all out in ANY and in MANY ways that was

possible, just to make you all comfortable, knowledgeable

and well of, but do all of you all notice of that? NO, the

answer is absolutely NO!! And that there is absolutely sad

and sickening too, but hey!! There will be a day coming

too, where you all that I am talking about, that doesn't

and that refuses to acknowledge that, will want us, ME,

POPS, YAHWA, YHWH, THE HOLYSPIRIT, THE GOD OF LOVE; MY

LOVELY AND DARLING WIFE, THE MOTHER OF ALL; OF HEAVEN to

acknowledge you all in return too; it will not happen; nor

will it work, or go in you all's favor; then will you all

see, feel and also experience the horror of being IGNORED,

PUT ASIDE and NOT LOVE like you should and would like too,

or to be, for I will absolutely remind you all of what it

was like, when you all had and have forgotten of ME and of

your; you all's Mom, Sarai, for other things and beings;

also for things that will not help you; nor will help you

all to feel better about the situation, that you all will

be in, but, one thing that is for sure, is that you all

that have been there and here for Me, POPS, LOVE MYSELF,

YAHWA, YHWH, THE GOD OF LOVE, will definitely experience

real BLISS and HAPPINESS with us, LOVE OURSELVES; believe

me, loves you all will not have anything to WORRY about; or

to be SORRY about, for we will absolutely have a whole lot

of FUN under the SUN; also outside and away from the SUN,

loves; trust me, babes and my loves, Crystal, Sarai, Troy

and Pearl, you all will be happy again; that they will, the

world that is, will see it and will bear a witness to it,

that day, that is absolutely coming real, real soon, and

believe it babe, Crystal, that moment is on its way any day

now; so, love Crystal Yehuwdiyth, before I leave, I'd like

to say that, I love you too, very deeply and tremendously

too; also eternally; thank you very, very much for taking

the time out to do this for Me, POPS, LOVE MYSELF and for

doing this with ME, POPS, THE GOD OF LOVE, your old Dad and

God, who is here enjoying the MOMENT with you love without

the TORMENT of all others, that is , or would be keeping up

any noises of course; so love, it was and is a real

pleasure to had come forth to speak to you, the world and

to speak through you too; so, thanks again, for allowing

Me, POPS, LOVE MYSELF, to come on through, like the way you

do, by allowing Me to express Myself, without a limit and

with love; so, love Crystal Yehuwdiyth, my love, I will

definitely bless you tremendously and I am totally impress

with you love; thanks for taking the time out to finish

this here book of yours and of ours, love Crystal, for I

truly, truly appreciates it and is very, very pleased with

it too, the book that is love, I am so, so, glad that you

have remained focus enough to you finish this and to get it

out there; believe me, babe, this is what I have been

waiting for; also, I am glad that you will accomplish it,

for I, POPS, LOVE MYSELF, YAHWA, truly, truly meant what I

said to you; you all, for I will be shutting down some

things real, real soon; so I want and need you love; loves

to complete this part of this mission here, that is

absolutely very, very important; my babe, Pearl may not

think so, but it is, but anyway, if she doesn't wakeup to

this reality here, she will be absolutely sorry and will

have something to worry about, when she have to hear Me,

POPS, LOVE MYSELF, you all's dad and God, have to say I am

sorry babe, but it is too late, for you to complete this

part of this and MY mission here; so I want you and need

you to let go of it, she will not be able to be mad at Me,

but herself, for I have watch you shared this information

here with my babe; even mentioned it on more than one

occasion; she just seems to just push it aside, like its

nothing to think about, but the day is approaching babe; my

babes, where the time for this book here to be finish and

well put together; complete will definitely expire, and it

will; that and this will be what you, or you all will

absolutely hear from Me, POPS, LOVE MYSELF, for those of

you who don't, or doesn't take heed to what I am saying;

said from before this day. And so, love Crystal Yehuwdiyth,

I am viewing and seeing that you are putting much effort to

finish and to accomplish this part of this mission her, I

will bless you with the strength and with the ability to

get it done, for I see that you are not far from doing so;

so keep up the good, good work love; also of the love too,

keep it flowing and growing too, for you have done

absolutely a real fine job in putting this here poem

together; believe me it is saying a lot and it is packing a

great big punch; kick too, for it is absolutely saying a

very strong statement that I truly love and adore too, for

you have definitely made my day, to say that to the world,

to honor thy Mother and Father of Heaven, first, and then

the earthly ones second in line; that there love have

absolutely blow my mind, when I saw that you went with that

title here, in fact, every last one of them is absolutely

real beautiful and significant also; so love thank you

again for your time, energy, love and support; also for

hanging in there and for seeing this here through all the

way to the end of it; that there is what I call a real,

real success and a plus love; so thanks for honoring us

through your writing; also through letting the world know

to honor us, ME, Mister and Misses, LOVE YAHWA, ourselves,

THE FATHER and MOTHER of HEAVEN, for this is truly a great

work of love; believe Me, our book will absolutely SOAR

through every, every DOOR, for they will absolutely want

MORE; MORE of it; believe me, they will love, for this book

of MINES and of OURS is absolutely DIVINE and just FINE to

Me and for Me too; and not only that, but that, it is an

absolute GOLDMINE for every MIND, HEART, SPIRIT and for

every SOUL, for it is a GOLD that will not FOLD, but GO,

GO, GO and GROW, GROW, GROW all in a ROW, for the rest of

our and your books them love will absolutely FLOW too, just

like this one here too, for I will absolutely see to it,

that every work and works that I and we have put out there,

for the world to see and to receive, will <u>GO</u> and <u>GROW</u> in an

<u>ABUNANCE</u> with every <u>CHANCE</u>. For I am proud of you and of

your works too; also of MYSELF too, the GOD of LOVE,

YAHWA, YHWH, who is here and will come to an end here love;

so thank you very, very much for everything in general; no,

babe, we don't have to have a conclusion in this here book,

because I have already spoken from the very, very beginning

and even in the middle of it, the book that is; so, I think

and believe that this is good enough for Me, POPS, LOVE

MYSELF; don't worry, it isn't cause you have done something

wrong at all, it's just that I have a conscious too, for I

have said my piece in numerous parts of the book; so, I

will be absolutely lien and go and take care of some other

things that have to be taken cared of; that needs my

attention also; so love Crystal Yehuwdiyth go ahead and

proof read the book; get it out there love; I will see you

again, on the next episode of your very next book of your

CHOICE to add my WORDS and VOICE right into it; so, love

shalom and I love you always, forever and for eternity too,

take care babe and I'm missing you; you all a great, great

deal being altogether, but, anyway, we will be alright,

real soon; have a bless day love and thank you again for

the honor and for the love of course that is from you

always. For this have been ME, POPS, LOVE MYSELF, YAHWA,

YHWH, THE GOD OF LOVE, OF THE ENTIRE UNIVERSE.

(Crystal): Oh, thank you, LOVE, POPS, YAHWA, YHWH, GOD

ALMIGHTY, for your time, your love and for you, most

importantly; also, I thank you for coming through; for

sharing your thoughts with me and with the whole wide world

also; at large. Further, I thank you too, for your

encouragements; for your complements and for your support

too, that is never short, but that is always there; here

for me. For that, LOVE, POPS, I appreciates you and I thank

you; also, I love you greatly and tremendously too; so,

LOVE, POPS, have a bless day and kudos for your very

precious insights too. And so, take care and keep up the

good, good and the great, great work; works too; also, and

you are absolutely quite… quite welcome love. I love you

forever and eternally too; shalom.

(<u>POPS</u>): Thanks love, Crystal Yehuwdiyth, for your real lovely, lovely and real touching words here, love, for I am absolutely impress and real touch by them love; by you too love; so thank you and kudos to you too, love for your time and the love too; also, for you have truly, truly made my day love; also you too, are quite, quite welcome also; I love you forevermore and eternally too; thanks for the time and for the attention too love; take care sweetheart; continue to be my rhymester of love who is my priestess with love. I love you babe and thanks again, for completing this task here, for it feels real, really good to see that happens and comes to play too babe; so, don't give up and see it through love; shalom again. This has been Me, POPS, YAHWA, LOVE, MYSELF, THE GOD OF LOVE and OF THE HEAVENS.

Poem title:

"<u>LOVE is an AMAZING THING</u>"

LOVE

Is an AMAZING THING

That makes our hearts <u>SING</u>.

Also, LOVE

Is an AMAZING THING

That possesses a real special <u>RING</u>.

On top of that,

LOVE Is an AMAZING THING

That makes our hearts, to grow <u>STRONGER</u> and <u>STRONGER</u>; Also,

<u>FONDER</u>; <u>FONDER</u>, with <u>LIFE</u>….

And, by the real sweet things for <u>LIFE</u>, and that there, is

what makes <u>LOVE</u> very special and an <u>AMAZING THING</u>.

Furthermore,

LOVE,

Is an AMAZING THING

That <u>HEALS</u> and that <u>SEALS</u>

The heart with the most <u>VITAL</u> and not with the <u>IDLE</u> things,

Like with his <u>COMPASSION</u>, <u>FIRE</u> and <u>PASSION</u>; <u>WARMTH</u>,

<u>TENDERNESS</u>; also, with his <u>LOVE</u> and <u>CARE</u>; most importantly

with his authentic <u>ATTRIBUTES</u> and <u>TRAITS</u> that is <u>STRAIGHT</u>;

absolutely <u>GREAT</u>, <u>SENSATIONAL</u> and <u>EXCEPTIONAL</u>, and that no

one can <u>DEGRADE</u>; <u>DOWN GRADE</u>, but to <u>PORTRAY</u>, simply,

because <u>LOVE</u> is an <u>AMAZING THING</u>.

And, besides that,

LOVE

Is an AMAZING THING

Because He, LOVE that is,

Is a very precious PERSON, LOVE and KING

That comes with QUALITIES and with ABILITIES that is very

RARE, MATCHLESS and very PRICELESS; also, He, LOVE that is,

is an AMAZING THING, simply because He, is always NEAR;

THERE for us to keep us SAFE; moreover, LOVE is an AMAZING

THING, simply because HE is never LATE and that He makes a

great HELPMATE.

In addition to that,

LOVE

Is an AMAZING THING

Because He, YHWH, is the BLESSER and the LIFE GIVER; as

well the SOUL PROVIDER; THE UNITER.

And so, to say anything ELSE, or LESS

Would be a LIE that wouldn't FLY; nor go HIGH

But LOW, simply because AMAZING is LOVE and LOVE is

AMAZING, and an AMAZING person that is always BLAZING with

the RIGHT STUFF that is absolutely SMOOTH, SUCCLENT and not

ROUGH; or TOUGH.

In a nutshell,

LOVE

Is an AMAZING THING

Simply because He, YHWH, YAHWA, definitely

Comes with everything NICE and with the SPICES that is

always filled with the HOT and SPICY taste and touch; that

never loses it FLAIR and real FRESH AROMA that would

definitely wake you and me, out of a COMA; believe me, that

AROMA that I am talking about is the very sweet smelling of

LOVE (LOL...) and not TONY ROMA. LOL...

And, believe me, loves, I am telling you that TONY ROMA got

nothing on this, LOVE that is; why do I say that? Well, it

is, because LOVE is an AMAZING THING that is ABLE and

CAPABLE to season all THINGS, all WINGS; even all BEINGS in

the right way and with his LOVE that will not die, hide; or

that will never DISAPPEAR, or LEAVE, but that will and that

have always CLING and COMES with Him, YAHWA, who is the

AMAZING <u>LOVE</u>, <u>THING</u> and <u>KING</u> that comes with everything

over; above all.

And now, as I close out, I'd like to say that,

LOVE is an AMAZING THING, because He, YHWH, is <u>REMARKABLE</u>,

<u>AWESOME</u>, <u>POTENT</u>, <u>IMPORTANT</u> and real <u>BRILLIANT</u>; also, is an

<u>UNDENIBLY POWERFUL</u> and <u>SPLENDID</u> and <u>CANDID</u> Father, God,

Love and King, that <u>SING IT</u>; also, that <u>BRINGS IT</u> with ALL

and with <u>ALL</u> he's <u>GOT</u>; with everything that <u>BLINGS</u>; that

doesn't <u>STING</u> or has <u>PAIN</u>. And so, loves, that alone,

should let you all know; or understands why...,

<u>LOVE</u> is an <u>AMAZING THNG</u>.

Poem written by: (Crystal) Yehuwdiyth Y. Yisrael.

Preface for the Poem:

("<u>LOVE</u> is what's <u>KEEPING</u> us <u>ABOVE</u>")

So, shalom, loves; I love you all; praise

MR. LOVE YAHWA, THE GOD OF LOVE always; forevermore.

And so, ladies and gentlemen here's my poem….

LOVE is what's KEEPING us ABOVE, and it goes like this….

And so, be on the look out for it on the following page to

come and get ready to receive the blessings from it; so,

opened up your ears, minds and spirit too, just so, you can

embrace the goodies that will be coming to and for you;

all, big or small; even tall,(LOL…)just stand tall and tune

your ears and hear it fly; before you know it, it will be

in your; or you all's lips. LOL… And in fact, that is why I

will let it rip and to also take a trip; so, don't let it

slip and get a grip. LOL... And so, here it goes, I'm getting

ready to blow out those real sweet, sweet lines; rhymes at

this here time, and believed me, that it will blow your; or

you all's minds at the spin of a time, all you all will

say, is this, that I am right on time. LOL.

Poem title:

"LOVE is what's KEEPING us ABOVE"

My dear loves,

LOVE is what's keeping us ABOVE with LOVE.

Also,

LOVE is what's

Keeping us ABOVE the HATE, the NEGATIVITY; also, the

STRESS.

On top of that,

LOVE is what's keeping us ABOVE,

While He, YHWH, BLESSES us with the HOPE to COPE in all of

our times of DISTRESS.

In addition to that,

LOVE is what keeping us ABOVE

With <u>JOY</u>, <u>BLISS</u> and with real <u>HAPPINESS</u>

And, not only that, but it is, <u>LOVE</u> that is keeping us

<u>ABOVE</u>.

Also, it is LOVE that is keeping us as humble as a <u>DOVE</u>

And, while, at the same time, giving to us much <u>MORE</u> to

sustain us within our CORE and not with <u>LESS</u>.

Furthermore,

LOVE is what keeping us ABOVE The <u>DESPAIR</u> with his <u>CHEER</u>,

<u>STRENGTH</u> and with his <u>FAIRNESS</u> when all other things seem

to have failed, when things seem to be <u>BLEAK</u>, <u>WEAK</u> and also

<u>HELPESS</u>, and not at its <u>HIGHEST PEAK</u>.

Moreover,

LOVE is what's keeping us ABOVE

With his PRECIOUS and PRICELESS

SPIRIT of LOVE, that is holding us together as ONE in a

very, very tight, tight BOND, and that there, my dear

loves, shows that LOVE is not CARELESS; nor is LOVELESS.

And, at the end of the day,

No matter which way, you, and I, looks at it, or any

situations, It is, LOVE that is keeping us ABOVE the

CONFUSIONS, the CHOAS and above the ENEMIES ways and way of

THINKING, when our minds, sometimes SWITCHES and BLINKS

from RATIONALITY to IRRATIONALITY; as well, from time to

time, from POSITIVITY to NEGATIVITY; plus, from a SWEET

state of PEACE to a BITTER place of WAR, that sometimes

DAMAGES our CHARACTER and IMAGE; even deep down INSIDE

within our CORE.

And so, loves, as I ends here; after all, that I have

mentioned, I hope that you all can clearly see that, LOVE

is what's keeping us ABOVE with everything that he's GOT,

and that there, is HOT, INCREDIBLE and not IMPOSSIBLE for

LOVE, for He, MR. LOVE YHWH, is what's keeping us ABOVE

through his LOVE that is not from BELOW, but that is from

UP HIGH and ABOVE. I love you all; keep LOVE'S name UP,

HIGH and ABOVE always and forever; eternally too.

Poem title:

"LOVE MAKING"

LOVE MAKING

Is something so, so unique

And, in fact, LOVE who makes love has a very special

TECHNIQUE, that has no TRICKS, or GIMMICKS, but that will

make you and I, THRILL, BALANCE and SWEET; on BEAT; not

ILL, or SICK; INCOMPLETE, but that is SOLID; VALID, like a

real BRICK of LOVE that will always BE in the MAKING with

LOVE.

As well, LOVE MAKING,

Is not just making LOVE

And enjoying a hot sensual; sexual pleasure in the bed,

Or in the bedroom, but that, it is a way of DOING things

and LIVING with PLEASURE, KINDNESS; with TENDERNESS, and

that there doesn't absolutely have anything do with

BITTERNESS. For, to think that way, about LOVE MAKING,

meaning: to think that it is only consist of being in the

bed only, would be absolutely ABSURD; also, a LIMITED and a

DEAD way of thinking, by someone who have no HEADS up; or

no REAL IDEAL when it comes to LOVE MAKING; or to MAKING

LOVE altogether. And, I say that, because there are many,

many sides to LOVE; also, there are many ways to MAKE LOVE

and to let LOVE do its thing; again, I say this, because

LOVE is not LIMITED and the MAKING of it, LOVE that is, is

not RESTRICTED; nor BOUND, but real PROFOUND.

Moreover,

LOVE MAKING,

Is a system that works with <u>LOVE</u>, along with <u>LOVE</u>, for

<u>LOVE</u>!

And also, by <u>LOVE</u> and through <u>LOVE MAKING</u>; by the way, <u>LOVE</u>

<u>MAKING</u>, is also, <u>WAKING</u> up the <u>DEAD</u> mindsets to the

reality, that <u>LOVE</u> is <u>HERE</u>; that He <u>CARES</u>, and not only

that, but that, He's <u>NEAR</u> to help <u>SPARE</u> us from the <u>ENEMIES</u>

<u>HANDS</u> and <u>PLANS</u>; further to the reality too, that He, LOVE

HIMSELF, is <u>REAL</u>, <u>ALIVE</u>; also <u>LIVING</u>, and that He, GOD

ALMIGHTY, THE GOD of LOVE, is the one that is <u>MAKING LOVE</u>

to happen; to take <u>PLACE</u> under any and many <u>FACES</u>; as well,

in every <u>PLACES</u> and <u>SPACES</u> under any; or in many <u>CASES</u> with

GREAT TASTE, ELEGANCE and with GRACE, just so, LOVE can

continue to REMAIN in the MAKING without FAKING,SHAKING;or

SHRINKING; likewise, without BLINKING in and out; or

without FADING out totally and completely in the EAST, the

WEST, the NORTH; or in the SOUTH.

Additionally,

LOVE MAKING,

Is something GOOD, RIGHT and PERFECT.

Furthermore, LOVE MAKING; or MAKING LOVE is a commodity

that is absolutely SWEET; real NEAT.

And, as well, that is full of real amazing TREATS to SWEEP

you and I, off our FEET. Bottom line, LOVE MAKING; or

MAKING LOVE is a trait that comes straight; ready with a

whole lot of passionate HEAT; that is always on POINT in

any JOINT; in like manner, comes COMPLETE; to help DELETE

and to DEFEAT all seeds of HATE.LOL…. WOW! Isn't that GREAT

at any RATE.

On top of that,

LOVE MAKING Is taking LOVE, receiving LOVE, embracing LOVE;

pursuing LOVE with an open mind and heart; then applying

it, LOVE that is; at the same time, supplying LOVE ; also

multiplying LOVE with LOVE and with a real good

understanding that LOVE MAKING, is a righteous and a real

beautiful lifestyle and a style that you, we, or I, have

chosen to USE and to FUSE altogether in our WAYS for YEARS

and DAYS; also to INFUSE within everything that we do;

think to do; while we, you; or I, lets it, LOVE that is,

AROUND us and SURROUNDS us, without a BUST, or LUST, and

that there, is a PLUS for LOVE; for the MAKING of LOVE in

the process. For LOVE MAKING is something PURE; SURE; also

that is an absolute SECURITY for our SELF-ESTEEM; believe

me, that there is not a DREAM; on top of that, LOVE MAKING

is also a CURE for all HUMAN KIND, MINDS, HEARTS, BODIES;

SOULS and for all SPIRITS to remain LIFTED,GIFTED, LIT and

FIT, and not SPLIT in any way, shape, formed, or fashioned;

also, with lots; lots of AFFECTION and SATISFACTION with an

undying PASSION.

And that there, my friends, as I ends here, I will say that

the ways of LOVE and LOVE MAKING is a part of MAKING LOVE

with tenderness, loving and care. And so, enjoy MAKING LOVE

and LOVE MAKING with joy and with a PLEASURE that is

without a MEASURE, simply because it, LOVE MAKING that is,

is an absolute TREASURE that comes with much, much PLEASURE

for LOVE and for MAKING LOVE; also, for LOVE MAKING. For

LOVE MAKING is what's keeping us afloat, on FIRE with real

DESIRES and to INSPIRE us and others, to make LOVE; to keep

LOVE, first; not LAST and ABOVE with a BLAST; with CLASS.

In a nutshell,

Keep MAKING LOVE

For LOVE MAKING is the RING

And also, the KEY for LOVE to CONTINUE and to REMAIN,

MAINTAIN; even to continue to SUSTAIN in this real crappy

world of <u>HATE</u> that isn't <u>GREAT</u>, through this very precious

gift and talent called "<u>LOVING MAKING</u>".

<u>Preface for my poem</u>:

(<u>"THE DIVINE SEEDS OF LOVE"</u>)

Praise LOVE, THE GOD of LOVE always and everlastingly.

Hi, loves, my name is Crystal Yehuwdiyth; I am a poetess

and a rhymester of love; so, I would like to present my

poem called, "THE DIVINE SEEDS of LOVE", first, to my

Heavenly Father and God, MR. LOVE Himself, and then to you

all, out there; so here it goes; it goes like this….

Poem title:

"THE DIVINE SEEDS of LOVE"

The DIVINE SEEDS of LOVE

Is a very special SEED

That is FULL of LOVE always,

And that's whether it is UP in the HEAVENS,

Or DOWN below, still, the DIVINE SEEDS of LOVE will always

maintain its DIVINITY and SPIRITUALITY with LOVE and

DIGNITY.

Also,

The DIVINE SEEDS of LOVE,

Is a SEED that is not GREEDY, or NEEDY,

But it is a SEED that is there to help us to proceed

With MORALITY and with POSITIVITY, not only that, but the

DIVINE SEEDS of LOVE, is also there, to help us SUCCEED

with CERTAINITY; with a REALITY that SUPERCEDES and that

EXCEEDS any EARTHLY men, or women; or any carnal minded

people's EXPECTATIONS, PERCEPTIONS; or UNDERSTANDING and

COMPREHENSION.

Moreover,

The DIVINE SEEDS of LOVE,

Is a SEED that will help you and me,

To GROW and to GLOW mentally, spiritually, emotionally

And even socially and physically too; totally; completely

Without losing its CHEMISTRY and ENERGY, and that there, to

me, is a SEED that we really NEED to be well PLEASE and at

EASE with; while we are UP, or DOWN on our KNEE or when we

are in a very tight SPOT that is <u>HOT</u>, or in a very tight

MATTER, or a <u>SQUEEZE</u>.

And, besides that,

The DIVINE SEEDS of LOVE,

Is a SEED that only <u>BRED</u> something <u>SWEET</u>, <u>DELICIOUS</u> and

<u>PRECIOUS</u>, and <u>NOTHING ELSE</u>, or <u>NOTHING LESS</u>.

On top of that,

The DIVINE SEEDS of LOVE

Is a SEED that is here

To be <u>LOVE</u>, show <u>LOVE</u> and to be <u>FAIR</u>,

And not only that, but to <u>SHOW</u> that he, or she; or they,

That they are someone that truly CARES and that wants to

continuously SHARE their LOVE and CHEER above any MISERY,

or COMPANY that is not in HARMONY with LOVE, and also above

the DESPAIR with LOVE, and not with FEAR.

And, last, but not least,

The DIVINE SEEDS of LOVE,

Is a SEED that will SUCCEED, be SUCCESSFUL

And real ZESTFUL; CAREFUL in all its DEALINGS,

Just to keep all things in a real BALANCE and with the

GIFTS of HEALINGS, for your and our minds, hearts, bodies;

souls and for our spirits as well; also, for our MOODS;

FEELINGS. And I say that, because the DIVINE SEEDS of LOVE,

is a SEED that is absolutely INCREDIBLE and QUALIFY and

ELECTRIFIED enough to do all of these; those thing real

properly, correctly and divinely in order and real

beautifully; simply because it is a SEED that is absolutely

DIVINE and JUST FINE, and not only, because of that, but it

is, because it is a SEED that will continue to FLY HIGH,

MULTIPLY and not DIE in any GARDEN; ANYWHERE; or in any

ATMOSPHERE.

In a nutshell,

The DIVINE SEEDS of LOVE,

Is a SEED that is and was created for LOVE'S NEEDS

And for LOVE'S MISSION; so, loves, do you see and

understand why, LOVE'S SEEDS is so DIVINE and PRIME; is so

INCLINE with LOVE and for LOVE to constantly BRED? Well,

it's all, because LOVE is something that is not just

DIVINE, but it is something that you and I, cannot put out

of our LIVES; nor out of our MINDS; most importantly, it

is, because it is a SEED that everyone and everything will

forever NEED always and for eternity.

I love you all; remember that LOVE and LOVE'S SEED is the

KEY INDEED to help us SUCCEED and to be HAPPY and FREE

everlastingly; so, praise LOVE, THE GOD of LOVE YAHWA

YISRAEL eternally and forever.

Made in the USA
Columbia, SC
14 November 2024

46371824R00098